CAPE BRETON HARBOUR

CAPE BRETON HARBOUR

EDNA STAEBLER

ILLUSTRATIONS

TOM ANTHES

McClelland and Stewart Limited

TORONTO/MONTREAL

Cloth: 0-7710-8288-6

Paper: 0-7710-8289-4

The Canadian Publishers

McClelland and Stewart Limited

25 Hollinger Road, Toronto 374

PRINTED AND BOUND IN CANADA

For all my friends

in Neil's Harbour

who told me this book

contents

The road from the Cove approaching the Point at Neil's Harbour.

The Malcolms' white house has sharp angles.

Miss Laurie's motley assortment of hens.

Always wondering if her man will come home safe from fishing.

*The men on the wharf heaved ho and a swordfish
was stretched to the top of the fifteen-foot pole.*

A swordfishing boat.

A fisherman in a swordfishing cap is knitting a net for a lobster trap.

A man splitting cod on the wharf.

A codfishing boat comes round the breakwater.

*The road to the Lighthouse Point is
deserted when the men are on the sea.*

*The few Presbyterians in the Harbour attend
the white-steepled church among the spruces.*

The rusty brown house on the hill that
Maggie is leaving for a job in the city.

*Occasionally I see Tommy Seaforth's head
popping round a corner of the nearest stage.*

"Maybe you thinks we's lazy sittin' round stages like we doos?"

The government lightship brings kerosene for the Light.

STRANDED

THURSDAY, AUGUST 9

Now I'm really shaken. I've let myself be abandoned in the bleakest little fishing village on the north coast of Cape Breton Island.

I don't even know the name of the place; until an hour ago I didn't know it existed. I can't find it on the map of Nova Scotia, the tourist guidebooks don't mention it, there are no signs on the road pointing the way to it. It simply appeared on a sudden bend of the coast after we had been driving through forest from Ingonish, the spectacular village twelve miles south of this one on the Cabot Trail.

"Dramatic!" I exclaimed at first sight of the lonely clearing, "A stage set for Peter Grimes!" Kay muttered, "A desolate dump." Shirley suggested running in to look for souvenirs.

We turned off the dusty Trail to a narrower road kept from the rim of a precipice by a snake fence. Across a bay on a rocky point the white sides of a red-capped lighthouse were outlined by the blue sky. Far below us a strip of beach separated the dark water of a pond from the shimmering silver of the North Atlantic. On our left a scattering of bare-faced wooden houses staggered up a hill that hadn't a tree. Straight ahead, against a background of ocean, a mass of fishing shacks clustered round a couple of jetties along a stony shore. Bleached, windswept, barren, the village was almost surrounded by the sea.

We stopped at a tiny store where Kay and Shirley thought they might be able to buy long-visored swordfishing caps as mementos of our trip. Glad to be left alone I stayed in the car and brooded. I had been arguing with my companions. We left Halifax two days ago to spend a couple of weeks in Cape Breton but because the popular, posh Keltic Lodge at Ingonish couldn't give us accommodation we were rushing back to the city. And I didn't want to go back.

Kay and Shirley live in Halifax, only 300 miles away, and could return to Cape Breton quite easily. I had come 1300 miles by train from Ontario for a holiday by the ocean, and I resented giving it up because I couldn't have a room with a bath. All my life far inland I'd longed to visit a rocky coast, to watch towering waves, to hear them roar; Ingonish is majestic, the swordfishing no doubt exciting: I wanted to stay there, to exult in the sea and the mountains, to talk to the natives, to go out in a boat and catch fish.

Suddenly, far from the shore beside me and silhouetted by glitter, I noticed a little boat with a figure at the top of her mast. A man ran out to the end of her bowsprit; for a moment he was suspended, he lunged forward from the waist with an arm extended, poised, recovered, then darted back to obscurity in the hull while the figure on the mast dropped to the deck. The men had speared a swordfish!

Immediately I knew what I would do. I dashed out of the car and ran to the store. In its dim light I could see Kay and Shirley trying on caps. Behind a cluttered counter was a big-boned woman with a sharp nose. I asked her, "Do the men here go swordfishing?"

"Yes, miss, all but the old ones that go out for cod and them that don't fish, like my man and the preacher and..."

"How do you get out of the village if you haven't a car?"

Her nose went up and she looked at me over it. "We has got a car! Only three people here got one, the doctor and us and Gladdie Buchanan. I won't take the bus, 'tain't fit to drive in ..."

"There's a bus?" I was gleeful. "Where does it go?"

"To Sydney. In winter it don't run at all and you can't get out by sea neither, the drift ice comes in an'..."

"Is there any place here to stay?"

She looked surprised. "You mean overnight?"

"A week or two."

I heard Shirley gasp. The woman turned from me. "I won't take you. I got nothin' against you but I always say it's chancey takin' strangers."

"Is there no tourist accommodation?" I persisted.

"Mrs. Pride's got a cabin but it's full for the night. Laurie Malcolm sometimes takes a boarder but she couldn't take all of you."

"We don't want to stay," Kay almost shouted.

"It's a good place, there's plummin' and only four here got that."

"Where does Laurie Malcolm live?" I asked.

"With her mother and sister. Her and Katie is old maids, held their noses too high, fishermen was scared to go after 'em."

"Which is their house?"

"White one right behind this, the way you come in."

"Thanks." I turned to the girls, "Won't you stay?"

"Lord no, not in a fishing village!" Kay seemed outraged.

"It's not beautiful like Ingonish but I'm going to try it."

"You can't stay here alone," Shirley objected. "What will your sister say if we don't bring you back to Halifax?"

"Let her stay if she wants to," Kay was annoyed. "We're not her keepers."

The woman leaned over the counter. "She'll soon leave," she said confidently, "there's nothing for her to do."

"I'll find something," I answered and made a dignified exit.

The Malcolms' house had sharp angles, a gable running from front to back and a lower gable going into the big one from the side. I opened the gate of the picket fence, startling a flock of chickens in the yard as I ran up a path to a narrow verandah that crossed the front of the house.

My knock was answered by a faded grey woman, about sixty, who looked so prim that I wished I'd worn a skirt instead of shorts. When I told her what I wanted she asked no questions, she simply said, "I'll take you."

I ran to the car and joyfully announced that I was staying. Neither Kay nor Shirley said a word. I opened the door of the back seat and dragged out my luggage. "Thanks for taking me with you, and please tell my sister I'll write." The girls didn't answer; their profiles were as fixed as those of sovereigns on a coin. Standing in the ditch beside them I felt like a mendicant.

Kay's arm moved. The car shot forward. Its wheels spat dust. I was left at the side of the road alone.

As I watched the car disappear, I said to myself, "Good riddance. I'll have a wonderful time here. I'll go swordfishing and swimming and dancing, I'll . . ." I glanced at the lonely village; there wasn't a person in sight.

Slowly I gathered up my belongings and carried them to the white house. This time a different woman came to the door; she looked a bit younger, had greying red hair and black eyes that flashed. "I suppose I'll have to let you in," she said, opening the screen, "my sister Laurie never turns anyone away. I wouldn't have taken you, it's too much extra work," she grumbled as she led me upstairs to a little room almost cut in half by a sloping ceiling. Pointing to an oak wash-stand holding a large pitcher and basin, she said, "You won't need that, the bathroom is down the hall. The pump isn't working because the water in the well is too low so you can't use the tub; if you want a bath you'll have to tell us and we'll give you a pail. And another thing," she lowered her voice, "we don't flush the toilet unless it's absolutely necessary; for the sink we take a dipper-ful of water from a bucket on the floor."

"I won't waste any," I promised, "I'll bathe when I go swimming."

"Swimming?" She looked startled. "This is not a tourist resort; we don't care to see people expose themselves."

"I'll wear my beach coat."

She glanced sharply at my legs. "I hope it covers you," she snapped and bustled down the stairs.

12

Now I suppose I should go out and explore the village. But why? I can see all of it from where I'm sitting on the iron bed by the window. There's nothing but the lighthouse, sea and rock, the dirt road, faded houses, fishing shacks, and scorched grass. All I can hear is the surf, a cow bell, and the clucking of the hens in the yard.

I certainly won't stay here a week; I won't even unpack my bags. The red Malcolm woman is hostile, the fishermen might be filthy old men and I wouldn't be safe in their boats, the glitter on the sea is menacing; it makes me feel as the Ancient Mariner did after he shot the albatross. I hate it and I want to go home. My family doesn't even know I've left Halifax where I was spending the summer with my married sister; if anything happens to them or to me I couldn't be found way up here on the edge of the world. I'm lost!

I ran down the stairs, knocked on a door where I heard voices, and went into the kitchen; a very old woman was sitting on a rocker by a black cookstove at which the thin grey woman who said I could stay here was stirring something in an iron pot. "May I make a collect phone call, please?" I asked. "I want to talk to my mother." The old woman didn't even turn to look at me; the other one said, "We don't have the phone."

"Could I use the one at the store?"

"There is none; there's no telephone line on Cape Breton's north coast."

No phone! No communication! I'm trapped in a vacuum!

Stunned, I climbed up the stairs to my room and wrote a letter telling my family I'll be leaving wherever I am in the morning; I forgot to ask the name of the village, the postmark will have to tell it.

I should never have left Halifax, but throughout my summer-long vacation there I'd had no more than a glimpse of the sea beyond the grey city harbour. When an acquaintance of my sister mentioned two girls she knew who were going to Cape Breton and wanted a third to share their expenses, I leapt at the chance. I was so anxious to stay on the coast of the wild North Atlantic, to go round the remote Cabot Trail, that I'd have travelled with chimpanzees – and probably been less irritated by

13

their chattering than by the prattle of my erstwhile companions about golf and their chances of meeting a millionaire at Keltic Lodge.

I wonder what kind of story they'll tell my sister. I'd better write her. But why bother? I'll be in Halifax before a letter could reach her.

Dammit. Instead of going back comfortably by car – as I might have with Kay and Shirley – I'll have to take the rickety old bus over the road I've already seen. I'll miss the most scenic part of the Trail over the mountains. I wonder if I could get out of here by boat? I'm so mad and muddled and scared I don't know what to do.

One thing I am sure of: I'll never leave home to go adventuring again. This is the first time and the last. From now on I'll stay with my family and do all the things they want me to do: play bridge and golf, go to cocktail parties and teas, to beauty parlours and boutiques. I might even marry George.

But now I am being silly. I'm safe here with these spinsters and I have enough money to get home. I'll just have to pull myself out of this slump and accept whatever I'm in for.

I got out the copy of Tolstoi's *War and Peace* that increased the weight of my luggage by two pounds. "Well, Prince, so Genoa and Lucca are now just estates of the Bonapart family," I started. I stopped half way down the page and started again. How could a Russian soiree have interest for an outcast in a desolate fishing village? I tried a third time and read a bit farther. Then lulled by the sound of the surf and a cowbell, I slept till they called me for supper.

In a small room with a round stove and a corner cupboard, the two women, listening to the news on a battery radio, sat silently at either end of a table; my chair faced the doorway to the kitchen where the old woman was eating alone. "Mother hasn't eaten in the dining room since father died," Miss Laurie, the grey one, told me. "We always have dinner at noon but we thought you might like Neil's Harbour fish for your first meal here."

I was hungry but when they served me oily black-skinned fried mackerel, warmed-over turnip and spongey grey boiled potatoes of last year's growth, I could hardly swallow.

14

"Why don't you eat?" Katie, the younger one, asked me when the newscast was over and her own plate was empty.

"I'm sorry but I – I can't."

"Oh?" Miss Laurie sounded concerned.

Katie was huffy. "Don't you like fish? You'll have to eat it if you're going to stay in Neil's Harbour. We don't have much else."

I couldn't hurt their feelings by telling the truth. I said, "I like fish, but I – I think I'm homesick."

"Are you going to cry, dear?" Miss Laurie looked anxious.

"Oh no, I wouldn't do that."

"Then you're not homesick," she smiled. "You'll be all right soon."

It was a good thought; I enjoyed the steamed pudding that followed. Katie gave me a second helping and told me to go to the wharf where tourists like to watch the boats come in from fishing.

I walked down the road towards the lighthouse. Past the silver shingle shacks (the women called them stages) was a wooden wharf where the rear ends and bare feet of children were more prominent than their heads as they leaned over the edge, and a wispy little grey-haired man was piling up wooden boxes. "Good evening," he said to me, "you just come?"

"This afternoon."

"Never seen you round nowhere."

"I was in my room."

He smiled eagerly, "You stayin' fer a spell?"

"No, I'll be leaving on the bus tomorrow. I'd rather get out by boat, does anything from here go to the St. Lawrence?"

"No, *Aspy* goes the other way."

"What's *Aspy*?"

"You don't know the *Aspy*?" He looked at me in amazement as I shook my head. "She's very himportant vessel, freight and passenger steamer comes up from Sydney on Tuesday and Friday with everything we needs. Goes back Wednesday and Saturday."

"Then I'd have to wait two days."

"You in a hurry?" he drawled. "Could go to North Sydney on fish boat, comes every day to fetch fish; she ain't a passenger

15

boat, smells awful of fish, but she takes folks onto 'er that wants a ride bad."

"That would be perfect. When does she come in?"

"Any time now, you can speak to her skipper."

"Cheers!" I said to myself, "I'll be travelling on the ocean, I'll see the coast from a boat; that is far better than going tamely over the rest of the Trail in a car. It will be an adventure!"

I looked around. Entering the bay was a vessel with a sailless mast and a bowsprit like a diving board with a metal sort of pulpit on the end of it.

"Here comes the *'lizabeth*," someone shouted. "Gotta fish."

By the time the boat reached the dock there were perhaps twenty children, three dogs and ten men chattering excitedly in a dialect I could not understand and presumed must be Gaelic since Cape Breton was settled by Scots. The children, tanned scalps showing through sun-bleached hair, were dynamos in well-washed jeans or calico dresses; the dogs were shaggy Newfoundlanders; the ruddy-faced men, like broad-billed birds in khaki caps with visors six inches long, wore rubber boots, thick trousers, and flannel shirts; shyly conscious of the presence of a stranger, they turned away when their curious glances met mine.

As the *Elizabeth* scraped gently alongside, a rope through a pully on a post at the end of the dock was tossed to the men aboard. They did something with it that I couldn't see, then three men on the wharf heaved ho. A monster was stretched from the deck to the top of the fifteen-foot pole! I was seeing my first swordfish. It was stupendous! The body was round; the skin dark purple-grey, rough one way, smooth the other like a cat's tongue; the horny black fins stood out like scimitars, the tail like the handlebars of a giant bicycle; but the strangest thing was the broad, pointed, sharp-sided sword, an extension of the head, an upper bill three feet long! As the rope was slowly released, the men guided the creature down to the dock where it lay like a rolled-up rug.

A little boy knelt near the head; with a hook he ripped open the glazed membrane of the huge round eye that was uppermost. Out of the cavity ran clear, slurpy liquid. The child put his hand into the socket, pulled something out of it then looked up at me. "Want heyeball?" he asked, thrusting his fist towards me.

Ughghghghghghghghghghghghgh! I couldn't touch the fishy thing. Everybody was watching. What would I do? "Let me look at it," I hedged. He opened his hand and I saw a perfect sphere, clear as glass, about an inch and a quarter in diameter, reflecting colours like a bubble.

"Take en," he said.

I still hesitated, "I haven't any money with me."

The child shook his head, "Don't need money."

"You mean it's a present?"

He grinned shyly and nodded. I couldn't spurn a gift. I held out my hand. The boy placed the crystal gently on my palm. It felt cool and tender as a piece of firm jelly or a gumdrop that's had the sugar licked off it. "What should I do with it?" I asked.

"Take en home and put in sun and it'll turn roight hard," someone answered. "Be careful not to break en." I held my treasure reverently; it didn't even smell like fish!

Another boy cut out the bloody eye socket, looked inquiringly at me, then grinned and tossed it into the water.

"How much would the fish weigh?" I asked anyone who could hear me.

"Ower six hundred pound, I reckon," a blue-eyed fisherman answered. "He's some beeg."

"What does it taste like?"

"Don't know, never et 'em, we just ketches 'em and sells 'em for folks down in States," he said. "Don't fancy to try none o' the big ugly things meself but some round 'ere cut off a bit near the haid and taked it home and cooked it; they say hit's got a roight noice flavour to it, loike pork, not strong atall. Americans must loike 'em or they wouldn't pay so much for 'em. We's gettin' thirty-two cents a pound today."

I did some mental arithmetic. "No wonder you're so happy to catch one."

He grinned. "We be, but they's awful scarce." With a saw in his hand he knelt beside the fish. "Want sword?" he asked me.

"Oh yes. Don't you need it?"

He laughed. "We just throws 'em overboard."

The rough grey sword was heavy and felt like bone. The cut

17

end showed bloody marrow that exuded fishiness. How popular I'd be with it on a train in a day or two! A fisherman saw me sniffing. "Stick in ant heap and ants'll clean en out for you," he offered.

"How long will it take?"

"About six weeks."

The man next sawed off the head, then the fins, the broad black tail and the fan-shaped crimson gill plates; as each piece came off the youngsters threw it into the water where flashing white birds darted at it before it sank to the shadowy creatures hovering in beds of waving kelp. With a knife the underbody of the fish was ripped open. I wanted to yell, "Let me out of here, quick," but the faces all round me were bland as blancmange. I couldn't insult them by running away, so I stayed where I was and watched all the stuffing being pulled out of that huge cavity: like a gourmet in a nightmare I saw long white links of sausage, steamed puddings, buckshot, sets of false teeth, lumps of pink lard, clots of black jelly, and bright red claret splashing over everything – including my legs.

The carcass, washed with salt water pumped up by a gasoline engine, was hoisted on a carrier and taken by four men to the scales. Everyone gathered round to learn the score – six hundred and eleven pounds, marked with indelible pencil near the tail and on a bill which would be paid to the owner of the boat on Saturday night.

The *Elizabeth* having moved to her mooring, another boat landed a fish. One by one the lucky boats came to the end of the dock; the others went straight to the anchorage, the men coming ashore in dories that had been fastened to buoys in the water. Twenty boats had gone fishing, five swordfish had been caught, acclaimed, and lowered by tackle into the icy hold of the fish boat that had come alongside.

When I spoke to the skipper about giving me a ride he said I was welcome to leave with him when he comes back at three o'clock tomorrow afternoon. I thanked him and said I'd be ready. But almost as soon as I said it I wasn't sure that I wanted to go. Swordfishing was exciting, the fishermen were interesting, the children were captivating. I was enjoying myself!

A group of little boys leaned over the side of the wharf trying to catch small black fish with a line and bare hook; others darted here and there with swordfish tails and guts before they tossed them overboard. A tow-headed, tiny little girl, her white dress dotted with fish blood, got into everyone's way. The only child I heard being scolded was a boy with the face of a cherub and a mass of golden ringlets falling over his ears. Another boy, perhaps twelve, smiled every time I looked his way but when I spoke to him he jumped over the side of a boat, hid behind the cabin and peeked at me with one eye. A plain little girl they called Martha held an eyeball carefully in a bit of cloth. "Why do you put it in a cloth?" I asked her, afraid I might be ruining my prize by holding it on my bare palm. Martha hung her head, hunched her shoulders and turned away.

A plump teenaged girl in a jumper smiled at me then came close and said in a whisper, "Don't they talk funny here?"

"Are you a stranger too?" I asked her.

"From Louisburg. It has swordfishing but it ain't like this place, it's historical," she said proudly, "got an old French fort that tourists come for. I been staying here at my aunt's a couple of weeks, having a right good time; the fellows are keen," she grinned. "What are you doing tonight?"

"I don't know, what is there to do?"

"Nothing, just walk up and down the road. Come with me if you . . ." she stopped herself, "if I don't have company." She giggled, then added vaguely as she walked towards the shore, "I might meet you somewheres along."

The excitement on the dock had died down. The fish were cleaned, the people were straggling away; the sun was slipping behind the highest hill across the bay.

I went back to my room to put on wool slacks and my Grenfel jacket, styled like an army officer's tunic; when I pull the belt tightly round my waist, my shoulders straighten and I feel brave.

As I passed through the Malcolms' kitchen on my way out of the house, the old mother noticed me for the first time. "Where are you going?" she asked.

"For a walk," I told her.

"Looks like a fine evening," she said. "I wish I could walk." She tried to rise from her rocking chair, then sank back into it

19

with a sigh. "My legs won't let me go," she whimpered. "I've had three broken legs and no one does anything for them." She looked accusingly from one daughter to the other. "Even the doctor won't come to see my legs any more."

"It's rheumatism, Mother, there's no cure," Katie said gently. Then turning to me, "Don't pay any attention to her, she imagines things."

"I want her to know," the old woman scolded. "It is awful to be old. When I was young I loved to walk, I'd go for miles and miles along the shore and never tire. Now I can't leave this chair, I'm weak and no one cares for me. If I were back in Newfoundland where I was born I'd be happy and still young. Now I am a stranger in a cold unfriendly land and no one comes to fetch me home."

The road that comes into Neil's Harbour from the Cabot Trail runs near the top of the cliff till it reaches a store marked Alec Maclennan's, where it branches: the right fork, slipping narrowly between the fishing stages, runs out to the lighthouse point; the other fork, after passing the Malcolms' house, angles left and runs beside the sea.

I followed the left branch. On one side boulders lay between the narrow grass strip of the roadside and the water; on the other side, beyond a few square houses and a steepled Presbyterian church, there were grassy banks and rocky slopes with spruce trees growing in the shallow earth.

As I sauntered along people in pairs passed me and said hello. Men walking briskly alone muttered goodnight. Groups of boys sitting on the bank flattered me with wolf whistles; groups of young girls giggled and called hello – I didn't see the one from Louisburg. As I passed a tiny store perched on the sea's edge a man standing in the doorway said, "Hello dear"; realizing he meant me, I walked faster. Where the space between the road and the water grew wider there was a shingle-covered school, an Orange Lodge Hall, and a little white Anglican church; beyond them a shore of great stones made the road bend away from the sea. I didn't go farther because darkness had come.

Straight before me when I turned back towards the village, the Light at the end of the Point was glowing with a yellow flame. As I walked towards it I heard talk and soft laughter coming from the night. Dark figures approached and passed by me. Sometimes there was a chorus of whistles. Once I heard footsteps close behind me and a man's voice saying, "Come with me, dear." I didn't look around, I ran till I reached the houses near the corner. Their angles, sharp against the deep dark blue of the sky, were blacker than midnight, blacker than void. In all the village I could see only five yellow patches of light. But through the windows of the Malcolms' kitchen, a faint glow came from a lamp left half way up the stairs for me.

CHAPTER TWO

EVER BEEN SEASICK?

FRIDAY, AUGUST 10

The sound of motors woke me this morning. In the dawn light I saw some of the little boats leaving their comrades at anchor to skim out on the silvering sea. At seven o'clock more motors started and the rest of the fishing fleet rode over the bay.

After breakfast I walked on the Point to examine the gleaming white lighthouse with the balcony round its red tower; for a long time I sat in its shadow and looked past the wharves at the village – that strange collection of grey shingled stages and little wooden houses painted white, yellow, green and faded brown. It appeared to have no plan, no streets or even lanes beyond the main roads; funny fences made of peeled branches wandered round the buildings in a way that seemed to make it necessary to go through someone's backyard to reach someone else's front gate. Within each enclosure was a house with a gable pointed towards the bay, a wind-tilted little barn and one or two outhouses. Scattered over the slope of the hill, each place stood alone, one did not obscure another, every house had a view of the harbour and every house could be seen by those who came in from the sea.

There was little movement in the village: the occasional flash of colour as a woman crossed a yard, the slow roving of the sheep and cows and horses, the playing of the children round the docks and on the roads. And there was little sound: only the whisper of the water, the shouts and laughter of the children, the calling of the birds, the groaning of the bellbuoy.

I thought of home, the city where the buildings are greyed with soot, not silvered by sun and salt water; I remembered the rush and roar of cars, buses and trucks, the frenzy of parties, meetings and business, the noise and clutter of people, the flurry and worry that I've been so glad to leave behind me.

I crossed a rail fence and a stubbly common to the eastern side of the Point and sat near the hollowed edge where the water gently lapped the tumbled red boulders that stretched in great masses below me. For a long time I looked at the sea, whose blueness flowed forever to meet the paler blue of the sky; on its distance ships were sailing and white birds flew, on its shining face was calmness. I breathed its freshly fragrant air. I watched a rock beyond the rest, with water breaking white all over and around it; I watched a man riding alone in a yellow dory, gently rising and falling in the swells, oars glinting in the sun: he was moving away from the Harbour, rowing far into the blue, and it seemed a most wonderful thing. I wanted to memorize the beauty, to have it become so much a part of me that I could take it back to my narrow street in the city where buildings rob me of a horizon.

I don't know how long I sat there, quietly, joyfully watching, not wanting to leave, but after a while the rough ground beneath me indelibly made itself felt. I walked back to the road in a dream.

There was a man sitting in the doorway of a stage, a man with pointed, pixie-like ears and a one-sided grin that appeared when he turned my way. I wanted to speak to him but of course I couldn't: he was a stranger. Yet at that moment he was not strange; he was part of the world of boats and the sea, a dazzl-

23

ing new world for me.

I looked round for something to talk about. Lying near the stage were some odd things made of wood shaped like a giant wish-bone with a flat rock stuck through the crotch and kept in by a crosspiece. "Why do you have all these anchors?" I asked.

"Ain't anchors," the man laughed, "they's kellicks. We fastens 'em to the naits to keep 'em in place in the wahter." He was tying cork floats across the top of a net which, he told me, he'd knit himself, a little at a time, during the winter. "You think you'll never git en done," he said, "but like a man's life, if you stay at en long enough you'll finish." Then he told me about the fishermen getting up before daylight to visit the nets with great smoking torches on the boats: he said they wanted herring but sometimes a shark would get into a net and swim away with it, or a swordfish would be wound up in it like a fly in a spider's web, or the plaguy dog-fish would cut holes in the meshes with their saw-like teeth. Sometimes a storm would come up and the nets would be torn to pieces or washed away while the men watched anxiously on shore.

I listened impatiently at first, I wanted to talk, I wanted to tell about me. I kept waiting for a chance to start but soon I knew I couldn't, that I wouldn't, that I'd just keep on listening. The man had something to tell me. "There's lots to know about this fishing business," he said. "They's so many different kind o' fish and they all got to be ketched different: cod, swordfish, herrin', mack'rel, haddick, lopsters…"

"Lopsters?"

"Oh yis, lots lopsters round 'ere," he nodded towards a long scalloped row of traps made of raw wood slats, shaped like a quanset hut. "Out o' season now, can only ketch 'em from fifteenth May till fifteenth July."

"I've only eaten one lobster in my life that didn't come out of a can," I told him.

The man looked at me sympathetically, "Don't they set good?"

"Oh yes, but where I live we can't get live ones."

"Where do you belong?"

"Ontario."

"That's far hinland, ain't it? Ye got no wahter there."

"We have the Great Lakes."

"It ain't the same atall, they got no tides." The man considered me thoughtfully, "Must be hard for ye livin' away from the wahter."

"I've never had much chance to be near it."

"I knowed soon as I seed ye you was stranger in Harbour. I don't live 'ere neither. Home's in Rose Blanche, Newfoundland. Me and some others comes across every year fer the summer fishin'. Been comin' so long my old woman says she's goin' move over after me."

"Would she like to live in this place?"

"I guess, most all in Harbour comed from Newfoundland so it's the same like." He looked at the sea. "Don't matter where ye live long's you're by the wahter." He tied knots without speaking, then he said, "Don't know what it is about the wahter but seems like you can't never leave it if ye live by it; when I ain't been out for a while I keep lookin' and lookin', wantin' to feel a boat under me." He stopped tying his net to gaze at the horizon in a thoughtful way. "When there's storm onto it and we's fightin' fer land, I sometimes thinks I'll take a job ashore, but when I'm dry and warm at home seems like something really good happened to me out there and I can't wait to git on the sea again. It's hard to figger, seems like ye belong to it. Can't never git away once it gits hold of ye." He bent over his work. "I tried once to git away, went in bush fer lumbering; it were good work, good pay, I liked it fine, but come spring I were back at the fishing."

He didn't speak after that and I didn't need to talk either; he kept tying knots in his net, at times looking up at the water; sometimes we smiled at each other and the silence between us was restful. When I rose to leave him he said, "Come set with me again afore ye go from Harbour, I'm mostly settin' round here. If I ain't, anyone can tell ye where to find me. Name's Henry, Henry Rider."

I walked to the wharf where several small boats were tied alongside, and men wearing black rubber trousers, rubber coats and tweed caps or faded felt fedoras were unloading the fish that half filled the hulls of their vessels. They used two-pronged pitchforks to spear through the heads and heave them out to the dock: big and little fish weighing from five to fifty pounds apiece – they told me – with glazed eyes, gaping mouths, skins mottled; these were codfish.

It didn't seem possible to me that one man could catch several hundred pounds of fish all by himself in a few hours, but there were the men, mostly grizzled old-timers with honest faces, and there were the fish, visible and dead. "I'd like to go out and see how it's done," I said.

A fisherman told me, "We usually puts out a line baited with herring but bein's bait be scarce right now, we's jiggin'."

"You know what jigger is?" A smiling old fellow with twinkling eyes and a long yellowed-grey moustache handed me a most unattractive piece of lead six inches long with a hook on the end of it. "Ye fasten 'e on end of line and move 'e back and forth in water," he explained, "don't take long till you're pullin' fish fast as ye can haul 'em."

"Without bait?" (I thought of all the slimy worms I've put on hooks and the fancy lures and wabblers I've used to try to coax even one lake trout.)

"Don't need bait wi' jigger. Willie 'awkins there bringed in four hundred and fifty pound (at two and a half cents per), 'e's top line this marnin'."

The men go out just before dawn, they told me (as if I hadn't found that out when their motors wakened me), then the sea is usually calm and they have time to get a good catch before the wind comes up, missing less days in the summer than the swordfishermen do.

X-legged tables, black with encrusted blood, were used for splitting the cod: the head was left on, the guts slipped out and thrown into the water, the tongue, the tenderest part of the fish, was tossed into a dish for a family treat, slithery pink livers went into a bucket; a wooden box with handles at each corner received the dressed fish. After the weight was recorded they were poured with ice into painted boxes stacked on the end of the dock and covered with tarpaulin till the fish boat would take them away.

When all the fish were cleaned everyone faded away and I was left alone on the wharf with the boxes of dead fish. All the men had gone home carrying a cod or two by the tail for dinner; I had nowhere to go and nothing to do. As I stood by myself it suddenly struck me that dreadful things could have happened to my friends and relations at home, they could be killed and buried without letting me know.

I hurried round to the door marked Post Office at the side of Alec Maclennan's store. "How fast will a letter go to Ontario?" I addressed the pleasant round face I saw through the wicket.

"Don't rightly know." The man's voice was soft and slow. "Mail truck collects round four o'clock every day, an air letter should go pretty quick from Sydney. Why don't you send a telegram?"

"I didn't know I could!"

"Go straight up to house along the main road where you see the wires and my wife will send it for you."

Now I feel free as a bird; I can send and receive a message in a day, I can leave when I please by sea. Nothing is imminent.

Instead of leaving on the smelly old fish boat this afternoon, I decided to wait for a ride on the *Aspy* tomorrow. I tore up the dismal letter I wrote to my family yesterday, dashed off a cheerful one and mailed it.

On my way back to the house at noon I met an old man with vein-reddened cheeks wearing a shrunken fedora, a maroon plaid shirt, and a pair of trousers that looped between the buttons for his braces. He walked stiffly, his shoes scuffling the pebbles on the road near the Post Office. "Good marnin' miss," the warm friendliness of his eyes was like a blessing, "you stayin' in Harbour fer a spell?"

"Until tomorrow."

"Maybe you'll change yer moind and stay fer good and all when you gits to know more. It don't take long, Neil's Harbour folks is friendly, always talks to strangers, thinks moight be they's lonesome."

"I noticed that last night on the road."

"Oi moind how they done when Oi come," he nodded. "Oi don't belong 'ere neither, Oi come ower from Newfoundland forty year ago, ain't never went back."

"You stayed a long time."

He smiled, "Yes, Harbour seems roight loike home fer me now. All calls me Uncle Joe."

After a meal of delicate, morning-fresh codfish a few more

pages of *War and Peace* put me to sleep. The blast of a whistle wakened me. People were hurrying towards the Point. Not wanting to miss anything, I ran out and followed them. "Where's everybody going?" I asked one of the children.

"To meet th' *Aspy*," was the answer. Then I noticed black smoke and the tubby body of a ship approaching from the south. Her whistle had summoned half the village to meet her. She tied up at the first wharf, confusion and excitement followed: her gangway was lowered, passengers walked down to be greeted by friends, children climbed up and balanced themselves on her rail, deckhands briskly unloaded – cartons, baskets, crates, lumber, coal, pigs, were trundled across the planks and dumped on the wharf. People who had ordered things were looking over the boxes, others were just snooping.

"Look, 'ere's our chair from Eaton's."

"Ted Dowling's got new potatoes."

"Cove's getting meat."

"Come on, Alec's got cabbages, won't last long."

A horse and wagon scattered the inquisitive ones who rushed off to the stores to wait for the limited supplies to be delivered.

The ship's gangway was hauled up. Passengers along the rail of the top deck seemed to smile superciliously as she began to move; some would be getting off at Dingwall where the boat spends the night, others having cabins aboard were on a pleasure cruise from Sydney. The *Aspy* will call here again tomorrow morning when people who are leaving Neil's Harbour will be on the wharf. And I won't be one of them!

"Catch any today?" I asked a middle-aged fisherman who was sitting on a bollard.

"Nobody ketched none. Wind's too strong, all comed in early."

"I wish I could see you catch one. Do you ever take people out with you?"

He answered warily, "We doos, now and again."

"Would you take me?"

He rubbed the back of his neck and contemplated his boots.

"Well now, I'll tell you, miss, I'd be right glad to take ye but I only got a small boat without fo'c'sle; you'd be much more comforble in snapper boat, they's built special for swordfishing. Like them there." He nodded towards the larger boats anchored within the bend of the wharf. From one of them a couple of men were getting into a dory. "Do you think they would take me?" I wondered.

"Might be they will do if you ask 'em," the fisherman urged. But as we watched the dory was rowed away from us. "Who shall I ask now?"

The man glanced at the few stragglers left on the wharf. "Ain't nobody round no more but if ye gits down 'ere by seven in morning they won't all git off without you."

HURRAY – I was going swordfishing!

Thinking films for my camera might be a boon to my adventure I went round to the front door of Alec Maclennan's and found it the strangest store that I have ever seen. There was an open space about nine feet by sixteen surrounded by counters whose glass cases were filled and piled high on top with a variety ranging from hairnets and pills to ice creepers and corn flakes. There was no standing room behind the counters, which extended straight back to the shelves that lined the walls and at the back of the store formed a platform about eight feet deep – the Post Office.

The reason for this unusual arrangement was apparent when I saw the man whose friendly face had appeared at the P.O. wicket earlier in the day: one of his legs had been removed at his hip; using his arms like crutches, he propelled himself by shoving his remaining foot ahead and pulling his heavy body forward. When he reached the front of the platform he sat like a benevolent Buddah on a dais, only he looked friendly, with thick greying hair, rosy cheeks and blue eyes.

"We don't sell films, magazines, newspapers, or the like o' that in the Harbour," he told me with a smile and a shrug, "only tourists want 'em." Then he asked me, "How long are you staying round here?"

"I don't know."

He winked at a fisherman sitting on the edge of the platform and said slyly, "Might be you'll be looking for a man."

"Oh no, I just want to catch a swordfish," I answered and they roared with laughter.

When I announced my project to Miss Katie – who seems to be always running around the house with a scrubbing pail – she

"Why not?"

"You'll be disappointed. The men won't take you, they never take women aboard their boats, it's supposed to bring bad luck."

"But the man told me that someone would take me if I was on the shore at seven," I argued.

"You can't have breakfast that early, it would disturb Mother; and furthermore, I won't get up in the dark to make a lunch for you to take along."

"I won't need much," I said, "if you don't mind showing me where to find things, I could help myself very quietly." Grudgingly she led me into a pantry and showed me the box that holds the week's supply of bread. "It doesn't matter what you take, you'll be seasick anyway," she said.

"I've never been seasick."

"Have you ever been out on the sea?" she challenged.

"N-no," I admitted.

"Then you're sure to be sick," she triumphed, "everyone is. It blows hard out there and the boats won't turn back for you." She busied herself at the stove. "And don't forget you'll be with the men all day."

"You mean I wouldn't be safe?"

She stiffened. "Neil's Harbour men are decent, you'll be safe enough, but it's a long time from seven in the morning till they get in at dusk. Had you thought of that?" She gave me a sharp look and her face flushed to the roots of her fading red hair.

After supper I knocked at the door of Alec Maclennan's house. It was opened by a lovely young woman with long curls and a welcoming smile. She invited me into the kitchen where Alec was shaving at a large square table. He smiled when he saw me. "Got your wire made out, have ye?" he asked as he scraped off his whiskers with a long straight blade.

"I've got exactly fifty words for a night letter."

"You Scotch too?" he teased. "Elsa send it for her, will you?"

His wife looked over the paper I gave her then asked if I'd mind reading it aloud so she'd be sure to get it right. "No word from you have been moving around no accommodation so girls left me in fishing village no telephone or would call wire by return at Neil's Harbour telling me you're

30

WELL I MISS YOU GREATLY BUT MUST GO SWORDFISHING MEET-
ING INTERESTING PEOPLE MAY LEAVE SUNDAY FOR HALIFAX
LOVE"

After she'd finished clicking the apparatus in a corner of the
room and had removed the basin and mirror from her husband,
I told them a few things about myself because they were so pleasant and curious about who I was and how I got here. We talked
– or perhaps I talked – for about half an hour before I said I must
leave them to see more of the Harbour before dark.

"Have you went up the hill yet?" Alec asked me.

"You mean the big hill with all the houses?"

"Yes, you better go up and look around," he laughed, "that's
where the fishermen live, might be you'll catch one."

Joining the main road beyond Alec's house was a lane that
zigzagged up the hill; I had climbed part way along when it
forked and I stopped to reconnoitre. "Looking fer somebody?"
A slim young girl came up behind me.

"I don't know anyone, I'm just walking around. Where does
this road go?" I pointed left.

"To our house, would you like to come?" She spoke eagerly.

We passed through the gates of two fences as we climbed to a
rusty brown house in a rocky yard with a crooked little barn in
one corner, a privy in another, and evidences of hens, a pig and a
cow. We went round the back and entered a large square kitchen
where about a dozen people seemed to be at home.

"Who's Maggie brought in this time?" asked a woman with
wind-blown grey hair who was vigorously wielding a broom.
The question startled me until her blue eyes smiled as she said,
"Maggie's always bringin' in somebody."

"She's from Ontario, Mom, where I'm goin'," Maggie announced.

With the broom Maggie's mother took mock aim at the head of
a teenage boy wearing a swordfishing cap. "Git off that chair,
Gordie, and let the woman have it." The boy dodged and ran out
the door. At the sink in a corner another young man was shaving. Under the square kitchen table two little girls were fondling
a patient Newfoundland dog. One of the codfishermen I'd
seen on the wharf was sitting on a rocker between a big black
cooking stove and a wooden lounge built into a corner, where

two young women sat holding their babies.

"You's stayin' at Malcolms', ain't you?" A plump older woman with a kerchief over her white hair was sitting on a wooden chair beside me. "And how do you like it?" She didn't wait for an answer. "Laurie is the finest kind but Katie's another kettle o' fish; if you're too quiet with them you come right up here to Mis' Patson, she'd look after you good, wouldn't you Ella Jane?"

"For all I loikes havin' a boarder, I wouldn't take nobody away from Laurie," Maggie's mother handed the broom to Maggie. "You finish the sweepin' Maggie, I'm so tired tonoight I'm roight shakey." She flopped on a chair near me. "Got Wesley and the boys up fer fishin' and swordfishin' this morning and ain't sat down since." She fanned her flushed face with her hand. "Went on a little trip yesterday and had twice as much work today."

"Where was you to? I looked over here and didn't see you around." (The older woman, I guessed, was a neighbour.)

"Oh dear Lord, Maude, wait till I tells you." Ella Jane's vigour came back. "Mr. Carey come over from Ingonish and took Dolly and me to Dingwall. We had the grandest droive, went roight down to the sand; then we stopped at a restaurant at Cape North – just as noice as any you'd see in town – and he bought us a banana split." She paused ecstatically, "Moi dear, I does love a banana split."

Maggie approached us with the broom. "Why don't yous three and Dad go in the dining room and sit comfortable?" she suggested. "I can't sweep good with so many feet round the floor."

I followed the others into a room with a day bed and two leatherette rockers as well as a table, six plain wooden chairs, a small round coal stove, and a battery radio set. "Can't play the radio," Ella Jane said, sinking wearily into a rocker, "one o' grandchildren broke the switch; done it just fer badment. Now we got no music and I can't listen to the stories. Ain't nobody in Neil's Harbour can fix it. It will have to be took down to Sydney." She shook her head. "Ye scarce git your own half raised up when grandchildren come round and beat up on things."

"That's how children is these days, don't seem to know how hard we work to git things nice," Maude lamented. "I always says there's no harder workin' women nowheres than in Neil's

Harbour." She looked at me. "And I know because I been in Sydney to visit my daughter and I seen how easy they got it in town with electric and taps and milk comin' in bottles. Seems around here we's always cow huntin' and carryin' water."

"We got lots more cooking too than in town; bakin' our own bread and preserving the berries we pick on the barrens." Ella Jane addressed me too. "Then there's washing and scrubbing every day, sewing our clothes, knitting socks and mitts, making quilts, hooking mats – I ain't complaining, mind, I'm only telling you," she said quickly. "After having fifteen I got it fair easy now with only eight home and Maggie soon leaving. But I'd rather have all of 'em. Sometoimes I's roight lonesome fer them that's away. Storehouse seems near empty come winter." She nodded towards a window through which I could see a small square building near the kitchen door. "That's one thing you don't have in town that we got. Merchants ain't got space to keep enough for when the *Aspy* and trucks can't git in, so we all has our own stores. We buy barrels o' flour, and sugar, and molasses in puncheons, and we salt our own cod; when it's cold we butchers the pig and the boys brings home a deer; it's roight good when storehouse is filled."

Maggie came in from the kitchen and sat on the day bed beside me. "I got to go to work now at the hospital. I'd like to talk to you 'bout Ontario where I'm goin'; could you come again tomorrow afternoon?"

"I'd love to, thanks, but I'm going swordfishing."

"Swordfishing! Ain't you a brave girl?" Maude exclaimed. "Did you hear that, Wesley? She's going swordfishing." She shook her head. "They'd never git me out in a boat; I'd be seasick before we left the wharf." She patted her well-filled waistline and rolled up her eyes. "I been on the *Aspy* and that's bad enough, but they little fishing boats bounce like a rubber ball when there's a breeze o' wind."

"Wind's comin'," Wesley nodded, "forecast says nardly tomorrow."

Not liking the turn of the conversation, I asked Ella Jane if she had hooked the mats with bold colours and angular patterns in front of the day bed and rockers.

"Them and lots more. I loves hookin'."

33

"Do you sell them?"

"Blessed Lord no, who'd buy them things?"

"Where do they get the mats that are in the Lodge at Ingonish?"

"Oh them!" Maude exclaimed contemptuously, "I ain't seen 'em there but they'd be from Cheticamp. French women make 'em from artist patterns."

Ella Jane opened a drawer in the sideboard. "Here's one Ivey brought me from Cheticamp, paid a good price for it too," she handed me the fifteen-inch square.

"Look on the back," Maude said, "it ain't made strong as Ella's, them edges won't wear. I don't know why the tourists are so wild for 'em. To me those homemade dyes look right faded."

The Cheticamp square was fine as French tapestry, the colours softly blended in a beautiful floral design. I'd like to go to Cheticamp to see more and perhaps buy one to take home.

Before daylight was gone I said I must leave or I'd lose my way.

"Can't go till you've had some lunch; if you're scared to go back alone we'll send Gordie with you." Ella Jane bustled into the kitchen. In a few minutes an oil lamp was glowing on the dining room table and we were eating bologna sandwiches, fat molasses cookies and pork buns with very strong tea.

On the way back to Malcolms' Gordie walked stolidly ahead of me without speaking. When we reached the gate I thanked him for seeing me home and he said, "So long, see ye swordfishin'," in a way that made me think he didn't mean it.

CHAPTER THREE

SWORDFISHING ON THE DEVIL DIVER

SATURDAY, AUGUST 11

The motors woke me again this morning. I dressed in the half light. Carrying my shoes downstairs to avoid waking anyone, I was surprised to find Katie in the kitchen making lunch for me and voicing no objection to my expedition. After breakfast I couldn't help saying, "Thanks for being so nice." But that flustered her; she said, "I just hope you won't be seasick."

All the men grouped around the stages stared at me as I came along. They leaned nonchalantly against the buildings while I walked alone in the middle of the road, supported only by a form-fitting wind, my clinging cotton slacks making me keenly aware of my femininity in the presence of perhaps forty males all strangely alike in rough woollen trousers and leather wind-breakers. Feeling the stiff-legged self-consciousness that used to come over me when I had to pass loungers in front of pool parlours, I couldn't make myself stop to tell them why I was there.

I pretended great interest in the water until I reached the wharf. There was no one on it. I walked back slowly towards the fishermen, looking at the stones on the road till I reached them: I looked up at them, at all those faces turned towards me. I heard myself asking timidly, "Is it going to be a good day?"

There was an endless silence till somebody said, "Yis moight be." The rest just stared at me. I turned away. I wanted to run but the thought of my retreating posterior made me stay where I was to try again: "Would anyone please take me swordfishing?"

The men exchanged glances. Some of them shifted their positions. One, taller than the rest, said, "Well I'll tell you, miss, you'd be better off in boat wi' fo'c'sle. You see, we don't have much room in them small ones," he nodded towards the boats in the roadstead.

"You mean I'd be in the way?"

"Not exactly, but if she blows you'd git terrible wet," he said.

"Does it come over the sides on a calm day like this?"

"Moi jumpins yes!"

"And moight be you'd git seasick too," another man spoke gravely.

"Even some of we gits sick when we's out," the tall man said solemnly. "We's used to it but if tide's strong and there's a gale o' wind we gits awful sick."

"We's sometimes took right bad," another man echoed. Some of the others smiled and started to move slowly away towards the water.

"Oi guess we be goin' out now, miss," the big man said, "you wait round till skipper o' one o' them snapper boats comes, moight be he'll take ye."

Pushing their dories from shore, the men rowed into the bay where the little boats were anchored and soon I heard them sputtering on their way to the sea.

Four larger vessels were tied up between the two wharves. I sat on the fish dock till a man carrying an armful of kindling came along. "Do you think your skipper would take me swordfishing?"

"Got no skipper, we shares." He spoke gruffly as he disappeared over the side of the wharf.

Ten minutes later two men sauntered onto the dock; one was young, fair and handsome, the other older and friendly. "Will you please take me fishing with you?" I was almost pleading. They looked at each other, the young one got into a dory, the other said, "Don't expect to get back before supper, do you?" I showed him the biscuit box Katie had given me. "We don't like to turn back if you're sick."

"I won't be," I promised.

"Come on then."

Oh golly – I was going! They helped me into the dory and rowed over to a blue and grey snapper boat. It was called the *Devil Diver*. The name gave me a tremor. I scrambled awkwardly a-board.

The men had made the boat themselves, they told me. Forty feet long and ten feet wide with a Buick engine in the middle, it had a dory in the stern, a high mast with a wheel aloft from which the vessel was controlled, a fo'c'sle, fore-deck and removable swordfish rig consisting of a plank projecting twelve feet over the water from the prow, and a pulpit, a metal three-quarter hoop, less than waist high, to which the long pole of the harpoon was fastened.

We started at once. That they might spy a fish even below the surface of the water, the two men, Gerald the young one and Ea-ger the friendly one, had climbed the mast where they sat on rope-swung boards like performers on a trapeze, except that their feet could rest on a crosspiece, their arms on a bar. Another man, Jossie, sat on the wooden door that covered the roaring motor; he was the "sticker" who, when a fish was sighted, would run out to the pulpit, untie the harpoon and make the fatal lunge. I sat on the only seat in the boat, a little bench near the engine.

Soon we had gone round the breakwater, round the lighthouse point, out to the open sea, climbing the hill of water that rose to the horizon. I sat very still, very straight, very stiff. Though the water didn't look wild, the boat seemed to heave. I tried to think how beautiful the village behind us was with the early sun high-lighting the little houses, but the fumes of the motor were strong. I remembered that someone had told me the smell of gasoline always made people seasick. I thought I'd better move away from the engine but there didn't seem to be anywhere else for me to go. I clutched the bench with hands like claws.

The village became a tiny clearing below the great dark hills. The *Devil Diver* swung towards the south; the gas fumes didn't change. Jossie, relaxed in front of me, kept his eyes on the water. "What do you look for?" I shouted.

"Just like two black sticks, about so long." He held up his hands eight inches apart.

I tried watching the water for two black sticks – two black sticks – gasoline fumes – no, no – two black sticks – two black – gasoline – I stood up. But there was nothing to hang on to so I sat down again, clinging to the bench. "You might be more easy atop the fo'c'sle," Jossie said, swinging himself nimbly onto the roof of the tiny cabin and sitting on its front edge, his back towards me.

I got my body off the bench but hung onto it with my hands till I was able to grope my way around to where I could almost reach the fo'c'sle. I lurched against it. I clung to it. I tried to put a foot on a certain spot on the deck but it didn't land there. By clinging with my hands I finally shuffled to the rail of the boat. To get on top of the roof, which was higher than my head, I had to climb up the fo'c'sle's side from the boat's narrow rail, avoiding the ropes that ran from the mast to the engine. The water was whizzing by and very close. I was scared skinny. I don't know how many times I missed but I do know that one time I didn't. I slumped against the mast, breathing the fresh salt air.

Then I lay down, my eyes closed, my head on my outstretched arms, both hands clenching the edge of the roof, my body rigid. I felt dizzy. I thought *This is it!* But nothing happened. I waited. I felt no nausea. I suddenly realized I never had felt any. What the hell! I wasn't seasick, I was just unbalanced. With the carefree attitude I try to achieve when I'm riding in a car with a person who should have his licence cancelled, I sat against the mast and started looking for swordfish.

How could I know when I really saw two black sticks among the billion sharp points of water that raised themselves capriciously round us? Dozens of those impish little wavelets deliberately deceived me as they danced up from the surface, imitated the curving fins, posed long enough to give me a thrill, then mercifully disappeared before I could shout what I believed I had discovered.

Because the men had been kind enough to take me with them I felt duty bound to keep looking at that disconcerting water, but my eyes strayed constantly to the stability and beauty of the shore. We were perhaps five miles from land and by simply turning my head I could see forty miles from the misty purple form of Cape Smokey in the south to fainter, farther Money Point which marked the northern tip of Cape Breton Island. Closest to us was a wall of red rock with the dark green mass of mountains behind it. The village we had left was merely a break in the surrounding greenery. The magnificent three-clawed setting of Ingonish was before us when the boat made a huge arc and started northward.

The smaller fishing boats, weaving back and forth inshore, shone white, red, green and grey with the sun against them in the deep blue water; the snapper boats and sailing vessels from Newfoundland were silhouetted in the gleam between us and the horizon; sometimes they passed near us and I held my breath as I saw three or four men on a mast sway five feet to the right, five feet to the left, to and fro, to and fro, like an inverted pendulum. Once we came close to another craft whose men shouted something that sounded like " 'ave 'e arn?" Jossie shook his head, yelling unmistakeably, "Narn." I asked him what it meant. "Have we got some and we ain't," he said.

Jossie – short, sturdy, with fine regular features, his face ruddy, his eyes blue – was an uncommunicative man: sitting in front of me looking over the water he didn't talk at all unless I called to him. The men aloft were silent too as they searched the rolling water. I wondered what they were thinking as they sat motionless hour after hour, watching, waiting; I wondered when we'd spy a basking swordfish; I wondered why I hadn't stayed comfortably ashore instead of subjecting myself to the pitching of the *Devil Diver*.

At twelve o'clock Jossie went into the fo's'cle. Smoke soon came out of the thin stack beside me and Eager came down from the mast. "Eatin' time," he said as he swung past me. I carefully felt my way to the bench where I'd left my biscuit box.

The door of the cabin was open and Eager called, "Have some tea?"

"No, thanks," I said, "but I'd like to look in if you don't mind." His "Come on in," was so enthusiastic that I wondered for a silly second if I should be nervous. The men, crouched on two of the three narrow bunks, were eating canned beans and eggs that had been fried on a cunning little square wood-burning stove in a corner.

"How do you feel?" Eager asked me.

"I think I'm all right. When will I know that I won't be seasick?"

He laughed. "If you weren't you won't be. You're doin' right good."

But Jossie said, "Remember time Jim Clipper had that girl out in 'is boat? She climbed the mast and ran round the deck like a cat."

I clung my way back to the bench by the smelly old engine and opened my lunch box. In it was a cheese sandwich and a crumbly muffin; I ate them both, opened a medicine bottle of water, drank very little, then climbed back to my lookout before the men returned to their positions.

There were no clouds in the sky. The sun was warm but because the wind was growing stronger I buttoned my jacket over my sweater and tucked my legs under me. I watched the water, the little dark wavelets more fickle than ever.

"FISH!"

Jossie was looking excitedly at the men on the mast who were pointing ahead and shouting, "Look, look."

"I see 'im," Jossie cried, running nimbly to the pulpit. I couldn't see anything but those damn points of water. Holding to the mast I stood up and saw the precious fins, two black sticks, eight inches long. Jossie unfastened the harpoon. He leaned against the iron hoop. The engine was switched off. We were close. Jossie was poised to strike.

"Aw – a trick," he yelled and we all saw that the two black fins were fastened to a piece of board. The men laughed about it but I didn't think it was funny. "Anyway, now you know what the fins look like when they're outa the water," Jossie said to me.

We settled down again after that and even I didn't stop watching the waves forming and disappearing. Sometimes the boat went towards the south, then straight towards the horizon, northeast, due north, south again, always moving, her men and I watching, waiting, hoping. The same anxiety was in a hundred vessels that searched the sea as we did.

Around three o'clock I realized why I had been advised to go out in a boat with a fo'c'sle. I thought up genteel ways in which I could break the news to Jossie. I thought how unapproachable he looked as he sat staring at the water. I thought how ridiculous it was to be so prudish. For about an hour I tried to forget. When I knew I couldn't sit still another minute, Gerald, the curly-headed blond lad, came down from the mast and sat beside me. "How do you like swordfishing?" he asked.

"Fine."

"Never been out before, eh?"

"No."

"Want to go out with us again?" He gave me a sideways glance.

"Sure."

"What's your name?"

"Where do you belong?"

"How long are you staying in Harbour?"

"Where are you staying at?"

I answered his questions briefly, hoping he'd go aloft. He asked me if I'd like a cigarette.

"Don't you smoke?" He looked surprised. "Not many city girls don't smoke." He painstakingly rolled a cigarette, lighted it carefully behind his hands, blew the smoke out slowly and settled himself to enjoy it. "Nice day out on the water," he said, "though it's gettin' loppy."

I couldn't stand it any longer; I said, "I'm sorry, but I think I'm going to have to embarrass you..."

"What did you say?"

"I'm sorry, but I think I'm going to have to . . ." I stopped. I swallowed, I felt hot, I knew I was blushing. He looked at me sharply. I glared back and cried, "Have you got an old can I could take into the fo'c'sle?"

He didn't say a word; he went right to the stern, came back, without looking at me thrust a battered tin pail into my hand then swung himself aloft. I slipped into the boat's little bit of seclusion and closed the sliding door.

41

Then, of all times, I heard, "FISH!"

The motor was stopped. Now, now, they would catch a swordfish. I zipped out of the cabin. Jossie was in the pulpit, the harpoon in his hand. I looked frantically where I thought he was looking but I couldn't see the fish. I couldn't climb quickly enough to the roof of the fo'c'sle. I thought I'd miss the whole thing. I leaned so far over the rail I almost tipped overboard.

Jossie dropped his arms. "Goddam shark," he said. I saw it just as it disappeared: two broad fins above the water. Jossie's shoulders drooped. He fastened the harpoon to the pulpit.

For another hour we searched the sea. The wind grew stronger and the water rougher. I wanted desperately to go back to a still, warm bit of land. I was certain we wouldn't see a swordfish. The men seemed gloomy too. At half-past five they turned the *Devil Diver* towards the Harbour's lighthouse.

We rounded the government wharf and tied up where we'd gone aboard in the morning instead of proudly running up to the fish dock. The men didn't speak. I said, "I'm sorry we didn't get one, I hope I didn't bring you bad luck."

"No, no, not a good day, too loppy," Eager said.

"How much do I owe you?" I asked.

Jossie looked at me sharply. "Nothin'," he growled and disappeared over the rail. Embarrassed because I'd offered money for generosity, I climbed up onto the dock and walked slowly to the house.

Is there any attitude of dejection more obvious than that of someone who has fished all day and caught no fish? Before I could speak to Miss Laurie in the front yard, she said, "Too bad you didn't have any luck, but here's something for you." She handed me an envelope, a telegram from home. I ripped it open and read, "HAVE FUN BRING BACK A SWORDFISH WE'RE FINE LOVE YOU"

"I'll have to go fishing again," I told the Malcolms, "I'll have to stay longer." Miss Laurie said she'd keep me and Katie didn't seem to mind.

I ran upstairs to unpack my bags and change for supper; I put on my beloved turquoise satin robe and felt sleek and glamorous till I saw in the mirror that my face was the shade of first-grade red salmon. I dabbed on suntan lotion and floated downstairs to stuff myself with baked beans, homemade brown bread and blueberry pie.

My message from home made me so happy that I wanted to celebrate – but there wasn't a single celebrating thing that I could do. There wasn't even an ice cream cone to be bought in the Harbour. What a place to live!

The Maclennans, sitting quietly on their porch steps, invited me to sit with them. We watched three kittens playing in the grass and the fishermen in a grey group on the bank above the mooring: "What do they talk about when they sit together like that?" I wondered aloud.

"I don't rightly know," Alec said. "I guess they just yarn away."

Soon the village was alive with people walking on the road, calling to each other and to Elsa and Alec if they happened to look our way. Gradually a crowd gathered in front of Alec's store and I wondered why they were there.

"Waiting for the bus," Elsa told me. "It's an hour late tonight."

"Are they all getting on or expecting someone?"

"Laws no, girl," Elsa laughed. "They just come down to see who might be coming in, that's the only excitement around here on a Saturday night. You'll see, they'll all disappear as soon as the bus goes out again."

"Where will they go?"

"The old ones will go home to bed, the young ones will walk to the Cove and back a few times, looking for romance." Alec grinned.

"Where's the Cove?"

"About a mile up north shore," he told me. "Used to be Hungry Cove. It's called New Haven now. You don't want to miss it."

But like all the old fisherman I went meekly and wearily to my bed at nine o'clock – on a Saturday night!

CHAPTER FOUR

I DRAWS LOTSA BOATS

Sunday, August 12

Because the motors were still this morning I slept till eight-thirty, when Katie knocked on my door and asked if I wanted to have breakfast in bed. I took the hint and dressed at once.

Whenever I don't know what to do the lighthouse attracts me to the Point. A huge tourist bus was there with members of the American Camera Club on a tour of Nova Scotia; one of them told me their leader is the best judge of colour in America and he thought this place the finest they have struck. With tripods and fancy equipment, photographers swarmed all over the shore, but none of them got the shot I'd like to have taken of a group of young fishermen in bright plaid shirts playing poker under the ramp from the wharf to the warehouse, with a tarpaulin draped over the side that is exposed to the wind and the women of the Harbour.

Lacking film for my camera I must memorize, or sketch, the pictures I want to take home with me. Although I've drawn nothing since the maple leaves and bulrushes I ruined in art classes at Public School, I opened my notebook and tried to draw a snapper boat. Beginning with the mast and expanding the hull both ways, it ran off the page fore and aft; then I drew the ends first: the result was thin and flat as a sardine can instead of like the graceful craft in the bay.

"Artist here last week drawed them snapper boats right handsome." A fisherman was looking over my shoulder. My pencil froze. "I'm not any good at it," I said – as if he couldn't see that – "but I want a picture of a swordfishing boat to show my friends at home and I can't get film for my camera."

"That's my boat," he said.

"Oh, well, do you mind?"

"No, no get on with it if you like, only I got some snapshots of 'er up to the house, if ye go up there they'll let ye have one, last house towards Trail. Just ask my girl for it, tell 'er I sent ye."

"Thank you." I knew I couldn't be bold enough to do what he suggested, nor could I go on desecrating his vessel in the face of his kind offer. I closed my book. "Are you going fishing?" I asked.

"No, Neil's Harbour men don't fish on Sunday, I'm taking my boat to Dingwall; forecast says wind's coming up strong."

"What's at Dingwall?"

"A safe harbour; we can't leave snapper boats here, if a gale o' wind comes they'd be smashed to kindling. Small boats can be hauled ashore but big ones have to go to Harbour till it's cam again. Might sit all week, we never know."

"What will you do all that time?"

"Fish is coming this way now so there's hundreds o' boats in Dingwall from far away and all over; we visit back and forth, play poker, do a little drinking. Time passes easy enough."

"It sounds like fun."

"It is so." He grinned. "And a good chance to git clear of our women."

We were silent for a moment while I was thinking that I'd like to see the boats in Dingwall and the mats in Cheticamp.

Actually I'm becoming so interested in Neil's Harbour that I wouldn't mind staying longer. I must catch a swordfish and I want to catch some cod; I'd like to taste a lobster – though it is illegal. I want to hear the men talk when they sit around the stages, to get pictures of the things I like to look at: the Light standing high against the sky, the bay with boats pointing to the wind, the jagged rocks with waves breaking over them, the houses scattered in the clearing, the Presbyterian steeple rising white against the dark and distant hills.

I don't know how I could have thought Neil's Harbour was barren on the day I came here. An artist would revel in the clustered angles of the little gabled buildings, in the design of derelict rowboats, coils of rope, kellicks, lobster traps, rust-rimmed barrels, pieces of spar, red, green and yellow bobbers hanging on walls of silver shingle.

I was making a few lines in my notebook to suggest the houses of the village when I felt someone watching. A little boy, perhaps six, with fair hair and dark eyes, shyly wound his one leg round the other. I asked him if he ever did any drawing.

"I draws boats, lotsa boats," he said, coming nearer, "and I makes 'em outa wood too. Made dory one time. But Richard made right good snapper boat wi' fo'c'sle and rig."

"Who's Richard?"

" 'e's me huncle, 'e's goin' to Hontario next week, goin' for job. Fishin's no good for he now, can't git no money." The little boy sat on a rock beside me.

"What are you going to do when you're big?" I asked him.

"Oh go away, git some work. Maybe in Pleasant Bay, they got steam shovel there goes round diggin' up sand right nice; Donaldybee Macdonald lives into Cape North 'e told me. Do you know he? 'e's me huncle too," he smiled, "and Tom Buffet lives in red 'ouse behind we, 'e's one, and in Cove I got huncle Willie. I got some into Glace Bay too, huncle Merdick and huncle Roddie, and we's got lots more 'ere belong to we." He turned towards me, " 'ave you got some?"

I shook my head. The dark eyes of the little boy were concerned. "Haven't you got nobody?"

"Far away I have."

"Have ye got yer mum?"

"Yes."

He smiled with relief, then pointed, "I got mine too, right

46

down dere in 'ouse behind Cranky Katie and Laurie and th' old witch woman where you's livin' at."

Whenever people ask me and I tell them I am staying at the Malcolms' they say, "Laurie is an awful fine woman, but how can ye get on with Katie and the old woman?" I think the daughters are not unlike Martha and Mary in the Bible. Katie would sacrifice everything for cleanliness and order, she snorts as she hurries about her constant scrubbing and carrying of firewood and water. Her first reaction to everything is negative, but I've noticed that she always does the things she protests against and is doubly generous by way of compensation. When a sailor who came to see a girl in the Harbour asked if he might sleep here she said she wouldn't consider it, but when he came back and said his girl was away with someone else and he had no place to go, she fixed up the couch in the parlour and cooked him a meal as well.

Miss Laurie with her faded blue eyes, her pale skin, her once blonde hair, is like a misty grey day when sharp edges are softened and things seem to flow into one another. Everything she says and everything she does is kind as she quietly takes care of her mother, her cow and her amusing assortment of chickens. She looked shy and sweet today when she carried her hymn book to church, wearing a pale blue dress that made her eyes look bluer and a black straw hat set straight over her greying hair which she had crimped for the only outing she allows herself all week.

The dominant person in the household is the mother, who is eighty-nine and sits all day in the rocking chair by the kitchen stove, her hard-wood cane beside her. She is accustomed to commanding. Because its look in repose is that of discontented brooding, I like to watch her wrinkled face for the rare times when a smile softens the strong lines that give it beauty. She must once have been tall but her body is now shrunken and bent. She wears a long dark cotton dress and a light print apron over which she keeps wringing her blue-veined, large-knuckled hands. Her feet in their high-laced black shoes never leave the worn linoleum in front of her, except to shuffle to the bedroom off the kitchen or to move painfully to the outside door to say, "Where is my pussy cat? Poor little cat, they won't let her in," though that ancient tabby is always asleep on the end of the couch in the corner.

Poor old woman, she doesn't see well, her mind is confused, her sense of time has left her, she remembers things that happened years ago and talks of them as if they were yesterday. All day her voice is heard in a soft lamenting cadence while her daughters smile at her mistakes and explain her frailties in her presence as if she weren't there. Then, though she claims to be deaf, she seems to hear and scolds them vigorously.

After dinner I decided to have a look at the Cove. I wasn't far from it when I walked past the bend beyond the church on my first night here. The road bends again as it follows the rocky bank then runs up a long hill before it turns to plunge into the village. There are almost as many houses as there are in Neil's Harbour, but the steep slopes to which they cling crowd them closer together round the narrow inlet of the sea. On one side of the road is a general store, across from it a lobster cannery and the still water of the Cove with fishing boats at anchor.

While I was looking around I saw the shy little girl they called Martha on the dock that first night. "How is your swordfish eyeball?" I asked her.

"It broked," she said and ran away.

"How's yours?" asked an older child who had been with Martha.

"It's flat on the bottom and wrinkled all over."

"They shrinks when they gits hard."

Rock-strewn and cluttered with lobster traps, the Cove is not as picturesque as the Harbour, but one place away from all the rest made me get out my pencil: clinging to the side of the hill, a wavy rail fence formed a triangle with a worn shingle house in one corner, a wood pile in another, and an outhouse in a third. Boulders sticking out of tangled weeds made a path zigzag to the road running along the edge of the water. As I tried to sketch, it seemed so stark, so heart-breakingly lonely – until five little children burst out of the house to play in the yard and a blond young father tossed a baby into the air with loving delight.

Beyond the village as far as I could see was a coast of tumbled stones. I jumped from one to another then lay by a tide-pool to watch lavender sea snails, pearly mussels, and prickly sea urchins. While collecting a few fragile skeletons I found the first live starfish I have ever seen: the top a pattern of pink beads, the underside alive with thousands of swaying tentacles. Delighted with the beautiful unresisting creature I wanted to keep it but the thought of its dying and fading – and smelling – made me put it back underwater.

The water lapped gently on tumbled rocks, fondled the hollowed ledges. I watched it and I wondered: will the sea ever wear the land away, minutely, eternally, bit by bit; slowly, with patience, on days of calm, quickly, with passion, in times of storm as a lover conquering a maid who passively yields to his laving caresses, inertly lies 'neath his violent lashings?

As I watched the white flight of gulls over the blue it seemed that everything I saw, every bird, every rock and creature, every glimmer on the sea, had meaning. What that meaning was, I couldn't guess, I only knew that when I looked at all those things they seemed to glow, and I to be filled with a kind of glory.

Till the emptiness of hunger urged a return to the Harbour.

The big able seaman who is staying at the house overnight looked absurdly pathetic as he sat on the porch with Miss Katie when I came along. He was boasting of his naval exploits and she wasn't believing a word. I perched on the rail to listen. "It must be very dull for you ashore," Katie said.

"Gahd yeah, and Sydney's the worst place; I'll blow soon as Doc Gladwin finishes the job on my chest."

"What's wrong with it?" Katie asked sharply.

"Nothin'. You never heard o' Doc Gladwin? Greatest tattooing artist this side the pond; his prick's no more'n a tickle. You never had nothin' done?"

Katie snorted.

"All navy people got a pig on their knee for good luck. I got some fair jobs." He showed us his arms. "Red rose and dagger, skull and crossbones, dove carrying a letter, a girl – look at this," he rolled up his right sleeve to make a nude dancer wiggle when he twitched a muscle. "And here's a bleedin' heart, Panama woman, hands-across-the-sea, my girl's name; a spread eagle here," he touched his thigh, "I couldn't show you ladies all of 'em. The sailing ship I'm gettin' on my chest is a beaut," he grasped the

49

bottom of his jumper with crossed arms, "wanna see?"

"No." Miss Katie's flesh quivered.

"I got a few hundred dollars worth but that's nothing to my old man, he's got about three thousand bucks on him."

"I don't know why you'd spend money on nonsense like that," Katie protested.

The sailor shrugged. "If I didn't spend it on pictures it would be gone on grog or women, this way I got my money's worth for the rest of my life and nobody can take it away from me."

Shaking her head in disgust, Katie went into the house to make supper.

"Are you related to these folks?" the sailor asked me.

"No, I'm here on a holiday."

"Who's with you?"

"Nobody."

"Jeeze baby, what are we doing tonight?"

CHAPTER FIVE

TRIAL RUN TO DINGWALL

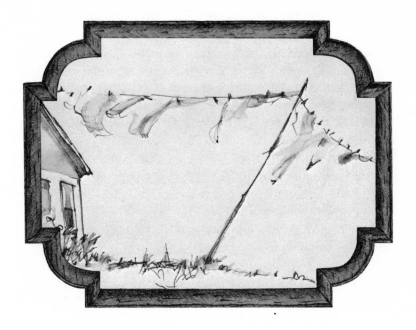

MONDAY, AUGUST 13

Wind fills the washing on the lines next door: round bellied dresses jostle one another like fat women hurrying to a bargain counter; pink bloomers are blown up like Siamese-twin balloons; a white flannel nightgown and a man's long underwear cavort with verve that is amazing in such plumpness; towels flick, hankies flutter, sheets strain to be free – and the lean tall woman who hangs them is a mast among flapping sails.

The men can't fish today; the boats pull at their moorings in water flecked with white, spray flies higher than the crags across the bay, surf rolls in broken lines on the strip of yellow beach, and over the rim of shallow water terns cut the wind with scissory wings.

From the shore children were throwing stones at the birds. Between the grimy hands of a little boy I saw a feathered breast, clawing feet and an angry beak snatching at a piece of liver held over it by another little urchin. "What are you going to do with it?" I shouted against the roar of the waves. "Tame it," yelled the one who held it.

"Can't tame woild things loike that," the other told him. "Let en go."

The hands opened, the bird flew free to become one of the many birds that glinted over the water. Swift, with white wings, black caps, red beaks and legs, they would dart at something in the flailing sea, the wind would carry them, they'd break away at an angle flying hard till the wind picked them up and rested them again.

Along the avenue of stages I wanted to hear the talk of the fishermen sitting on the grass, but being an outsider – and a female – I self-consciously looked away as I walked by them, knowing they watched me as I passed.

I went in to Alec's to ask him how I could go to Cheticamp. Alec seems to know what everyone is doing and planning to do. His store is like a club where people come to exchange bits of gossip or information as they lean against the counters or dangle their legs from the edge of the platform and observe what is moving on the road from the Trail.

Alec told me the bus runs only half way to Cheticamp. He said none of the three people in the Harbour who have cars are going down that way but there is a rumour that some of the boys in the Cove are having a car from Dingwall drive them over the Trail tomorrow to fetch beer. "They may have room for you," he said, "the only other way is to hobo."

"You mean hitch-hike? I'd be scared."

"You'd be safe enough with all the folk around here, of course you never know about the tourists." Alec's eyes were teasing. "There won't be many cars on the road, but you might get one to take you."

I made a daring decision. "I'll make a trial run to Dingwall this afternoon."

"A good idea," said Alec, "if anyone is passing the Harbour they have to be going there because there's nothing but bush in the twelve miles between us and them."

I went back to my room to study tourist guidebooks. The beguiling descriptions of Cape Breton make me want to go everywhere: to enjoy the old-world charm of Isle Madame with its gracious Breton ladies, to see the pastoral valley of the Margaree, lovely Whycocomagh, Gaelic Baddeck, salty Lac Bras d'Or, the giant MacAskill's tomb in drowsy Englishtown, the Highland dancing at Ste. Anne's; I want to hear the fascinating tales of Louisburg and Arichat, to learn the mystery of villages named Grand Etang, Meat Cove, Myra's Gut, Gabarus Bay, Main a Dieu and Chimney Corner. But how can I get around the island with two heavy bags, three coats, a smelly swordfish sword, and no private transporation?

After dinner I walked towards the Trail. Just as I reached it I saw a cloud of dust as a car came up the nearest hill. I ran towards it waving. The car stopped. Its lone driver was in uniform, maroon trimmed with gold braid. "What's wrong?" he asked with a look of alarm.

"Nothing, I want a ride to Dingwall."

"Hunnnnnhh," he snorted, looking at me sternly. "Get in," he jerked his head, "I'm going over there." He was a senior constable of the Royal Canadian Mounted Police, veteran of the Imperial Army in India, ahem. I felt very safe.

The ride through forest was unexciting till ahead we could see the white houses and spired church of Cape North snuggled amongst the highest mountains in Cape Breton. The straight sides of the Sugarloaf, sighted first by Cabot in 1497, was one of a line of peaks that stretches to the sea along the side of Sunrise Valley where the Aspy River broadens to Aspy Bay. We turned right, where great white mounds of mined gypsum were a startling anachronism against the dark and ancient hills.

Past a twist in the steeply climbing road we saw what looked like the top of a forest of dead trees; as the car rose to the crest of the hill our eyes ran down slim branchless trunks till they reached the hulls of hundreds of fishing vessels of different colours and sizes, all equipped with masts, motors and projecting runways. The harbour was a pocketful of boats so closely anchored that a man could walk from one deck to another round its rim.

There were schooners and jacks, ketches and smacks, snapper

53

boats and skiffs; from Port au Basque, St. Johns, Glace Bay, Louisburg and Yarmouth; from all the coast of Newfoundland and all of Nova Scotia they had come to kill the wary, wondrous swordfish which from July to September mystifies and provokes the rugged men of the rocky northern seaboard. Loving the sport, the gamble, the hope of fabulous luck, like men obsessed, they had piled up their lobster traps, hauled in their herring nets, coiled their codfish trawls and become rivals in pursuit of the monstrous creatures that warm their fins in the summer sunshine off the shores of Cape Breton Island.

In July the search for the precious prey is made near Glace Bay and Louisburg; when the middle of August comes the men on the masts follow the broad-billed fish to the fertile grounds between Ingonish and Dingwall where the long swords slash and the toothless mouths gobble defenceless mackerel and herring. By the end of September the roving gladiators disappear from the North Atlantic.

"Where do they come from? Where do they go?" the fishermen keep asking the unanswerable questions as they gather in the harbours at nightfall or when a roughened sea confines them to the roadsteads by day – and there are many days when the men yarn away the hours of idleness in the fo'c'sles, in the stages, or on the grass around the inlets, while the wind lashes up the water to hide the elusive fins.

The capture of the swordfish, divided by so many boats, is as uncertain as the weather that controls it. The smaller vessels cruising not far from shore, with only two men aboard, are lucky to catch even three in a season; the larger craft with as many as five watchers on a mast, searching several miles from land, may bring in six to ten fish in a day – or none. Since Canadians generally are ignorant of the delicacy of boneless swordfish steak, an annual average of a million and a half pounds, almost the entire Cape Breton catch, is shipped to Boston whence it is distributed to meet an appreciative American appetite.

There was little else to interest me in Dingwall, with its widely scattered houses: a narrow inlet where steamers come to call for gypsum, a huge dredge anchored at a wharf, and a fish dock where I was given a well-dried swordfish sword. "I got a sword for you too," the constable said when I met him as we'd arranged, "but it's a fresh one so I'll keep it for my collection. I scrape and sand them and carve hilts like those on famous swords of history; it's something to do when I'm snowed in." He took me with him to have tea at the home of an old Gaelic-speaking friend, then drove me to my gate at Neil's Harbour. Hitchhiking is pleasant and easy. Tomorrow I'll go to Cheticamp.

This evening people passed the house carrying boxes and coffeepots. I walked up the Cove road to see where they were going: into the Orange Lodge Hall. On my way back a toothless smiling older man, with a big pitcher and an uncovered angel cake, said to me, "You're goin' the wrong way, dear, there's a Time in the Hall tonight. Better not miss it."

"I wasn't invited," I said.

"Times is fer everybody. Tonight it's a send-off fer young men joined up for soldiering, can't make a livin' at fishin' no more. Come right along."

I thanked him and kept walking till I saw the girl from Louisburg with a young man. "You still here?" she called to me. "Going to the Time?"

"I'd like to but I'd feel queer going alone."

"My mother and aunt'll take you with them, won't ye, mom?" she turned towards two older women who came up the road behind her.

I followed them through the gathering of men round the doorway of the Hall into an unpainted room lit by two Colman lanterns where women and children sat close together on rows of benches and young girls perched on trestle tables around the walls. On a low shallow stage a man with rosy cheeks and a clerical collar shouted over the din, "Come up, come up here, boys," till four young men huddled together at the back of the platform.

The preacher asked us to render "Oh Canada" and a shrill soprano started us off. The clergyman made a brief speech about the bravery of the boys on the stage who were leaving to see the world. Three older men up front bared their heads, passed around their caps, took them to the platform, emptied them on a table, and with the minister leaned over to count the collection. The audience watched and waited almost with breathless suspense. "Thirty-one dollars and seventy-three cents," the mini-

55

ster announced. We clapped and some of the children whistled. The money was divided: the preacher gave each of the boys seven dollars in nickels, dimes, quarters and coppers; the rest, he said, would be kept for the next entertainment. One of the young men make an inaudible thank-you speech. We cheered. The meeting was over.

WHAM! CLATTER! CRASH! The conscripts jumped off the stage. Youngsters made a dash for the door. Women rattled kettles and stove lids. Men piled benches against the walls. The centre of the Hall was cleared, an accordian wheezed, a fiddle sang, and four couples danced a Square. Everyone seemed to be having a wonderful time as I watched alone from the sidelines.

A slim pretty girl wearing a cherry red coat came and stood beside me; her eyes were dark and bright as a squirrel's, her short black hair was curled, her smile was merry. "You goin' oop?" she asked me.

"Up where?"

"Oop stairs to git something to eat. Come on." She took my hand and led me to the private precincts of the Orange Lodge. Tables across one end were almost hidden by plates of sandwiches, cookies, cakes, and the aproned housewives who were serving.

We were about to sit on chairs that lined the walls when two young men pulled my companion down between them. "Bert, shut up yer silliness," and "Charle, quit yer tarmentin'," she protested, but didn't seem displeased; as they laughed and teased her she kept smiling and said to me, "Ain't them some foolish?" When we'd finished our snack she stood up and addressed her admirers, "Keep stuffin' yerselves, you gullguts, me and her's goin' git Fred."

"Aw no, Molly," Bert pleaded, "give us a chance."

"Leave 'im home and dance with we," Charle begged and each man took hold of a red-coated arm.

"Git out, ye silly boogers, them women by table is watching we," Molly shrugged herself free. "I don't want none but me own man."

She took my hand as we walked down the road towards the yellow flame of the Light. "Moight be Fred won't come," Molly said, "he don't loike dancing but Oi loves it and he wouldn't moind if I'd go dancing every noight, he's that koind." She smiled. "Long's I'm having a good toime, he never says nothing."

Quietly Molly opened the door of a little shingle house near the Point. We tiptoed into the lamplit kitchen where a ruddy-faced young man was curled up asleep on a couch. "Look at him, got into a case of vanilla," Molly whispered. "I'll let en be." She spread a blanket over him. "He's goin' swordfishing early if it's cam." Taking the lamp from the table, she said, "Coom, I'll show ye moi kids," and led me into a room with two beds and a crib holding a confusion of little arms, legs, quilts and tousled heads. "That's Philip and Arlie and Freddie," she said at the bed nearest the door; "there's Frillie in cot," we tiptoed over; "and Jeanie, Sandy and Gwendoline in other bed," we crossed the room to them; "and in our room is the baby," we had a quick look at her too. "That's all of 'em," Molly looked at me impishly, "eight in noine year," she laughed, "ain't that some good?"

Soon we were back at the Time where the young men flirted with Molly, who whirled gaily all evening with one partner after another.

A recruit invited me into the shadows to have a drink of rum. "Have a dance?" a young man asked me. "Nothin' to worry, I'll push ye through." A fisherman I recognized as the one who had given me the sword on the dock said, "Here's girl were leavin' Harbour two days ago and her ain't gone yet." Another asked, "When be ye goin'?" I answered, "Day after tomorrow." He laughed, "I don't believe ye will do." (At that moment I was never surer that I would.) Afraid to be friendly with men who were strangers, I started walking down the road towards the Light. Then a giant whose cap almost hid his face came very close and murmured, "Come for a walk with me, dear," and I ran fast as I could to the safety of the Malcolms' wobbly gate.

CHAPTER SIX

HITCH-HIKE TO CHETICAMP

TUESDAY, AUGUST 14

This morning I dressed to hitch-hike to Cheticamp. To definitely mark me as a harmless summer-holiday sort of person, I put on the same outfit I had such good luck in yesterday – a straw sunbonnet and a playsuit with a skirt that ties on and is open down the front. I carried my notebook, my Grenfel, and the lunch Katie gave me when she realized she couldn't persuade me not to go.

At nine o'clock I walked out to the Trail where I sat in the shade by the roadside to wait for a ride. Four bare-footed children carrying lard pails stared at me as they passed on their way to the barrens. A grey-haired woman with a stick went purposefully into the bushes below the hill. I kept watching for the cloud of dust that would tell me a ride was coming my way.

An hour later the woman emerged from the bush chasing a cow. Soon the children hurried homeward with their pails full of blueberries. I still sat and watched for a ride.

At ten-thirty a car coming from the Harbour stopped beside me. "Alec said you'd be looking for a ride, I'm going as far as Dingwall, d'you wanna get in?" I most gratefully did. The man was a travelling salesman; we talked politely about the local drought and the kindness of Cape Breton people.

At the corner where the road turns towards Dingwall I got out and waited in the dusty wind till the first thing on wheels came along. When I saw that it was a ramshackle truck with three men in the cab I apologized for flagging it. But the small middle-aged man sitting between two younger ones said, "We are going to Cheticamp and you will have a ride. I shall go in de back."

"No, no I wouldn't think of letting you," I protested and the young men confirmed the discomfort the older one would suffer if he rode in the sun and the dust of the open van. The French Canadian's gallantry was impervious. "I say no," he shouted a-bove the noise of the engine and the argument. "Alphonse Ducette will not leave a ladee standing at de side of de road," he smiled at me and bowed courteously. "It will much please me if she will accept my place."

I was not at all happy about getting into the dilapidated lorry but I couldn't spurn such chivalry. Expressing my gratitude and reluctance to accept the sacrifice, I sat between the men in front while my knight errant scrambled on the pile of old tires and po-tato bags behind us.

The truck crawled forward with a whirrrrrrrrrr. It climbed to the top of the long grade past Cape North village in low gear. The view was magnificent, I looked through the dirty rear window to prolong it; M. Ducette, smiling with joy, made the gracious ges-ture of a host proudly sharing his possessions.

The sea, the river, the villages disappeared as we rattled along; half way up the steep slope of North Mountain the engine splut-tered and stopped. The driver stepped on the brake. We moved backward. He jerked on the emergency. Crowding us on the right was a wall of rock; falling abruptly from the road on the left were the dark green depths of a gorge, mysterious and terrifying, a thousand feet below. A flimsy wooden guard rail promised no protection against the waywardness of our temperamental old crate. With some coaxing it decided to try again, complaining loudly and stopping every time we crept up an incline – and there was no end of inclines as we crossed the mountain range.

The men in the cab were uneasy. They leaned forward and shouted across me: "Feed line's clogged."

"Dirt in the gas."

"Never make it."

"Brakes won't hold."

"Better go back."

"No place to turn."

My muscles felt brittle. We were passing through scenery the guidebooks had lauded as the most picturesque in the world but I was too scared to look at anything beyond the narrow road.

When we reached a level stretch with scrub bush bordering both sides and not a bit of grandeur in sight, we had a flat tire. I sat on a rock beside the road and fumed. The noonday sun was vindictive, there was no shade, hot air shimmered over the Trail, which was dusty as a prairie in a drought. There was nothing to look at but the greyed bushes. And the truck. The blasted old red truck with its rusty wheels over which the men sweated and strained for an hour while I picked a few gritty raspberries, surreptitiously ate Katie's lady-like cheese sandwich and a very stale doughnut, and just sat, wondering how three men could be crazy enough to start crossing mountains in a contraption that looked like a mechanized rail fence and acted like a mule.

I wished I'd never seen them. I wished it had rained and I'd stayed safely at Neil's Harbour. I prayed that a real car would come along and get me out of the mess.

At last a car came, a big green Cadillac. The men hailed it and it stopped ahead of us. When the driver got out and walked back to the truck I had the chance I'd been hoping for. I ran up to the car; there were three middle-aged women in it, all of them wearing sunglasses, hairnets, and the kind of uncreasable print dresses that are perfect for travelling. They looked at me in my sunbonnet and playsuit as if I were a waif. I felt like one; a dusty, sunburned, grovelling one. I would have slunk away but I was desperate. Seeing their capacious comfort made me bold.

I told them that hitch-hiking was not my usual mode of travel – I wanted them to know I was really genteel – I told them this was the first ride I'd ever had in a truck; I complained about being deafened by the crescendo of the ever-changing gears, about the faulty brakes. I told them of my terror. I didn't ask them to take me with them, I just said that the men were talking of abandoning the truck and walking back over the miles of mountains in the dust and the merciless sun.

While I spoke they raised their eyebrows, they exchanged glances. When I stopped talking there was an awkward pause, then the woman with a bleach and too much rouge, said, "We'd take you with us if we had more room but we don't like having three in a seat when we travel."

That made me furious. It made me hate those damned superior females, those goggle-eyed, sightseeing snobs with the humanity of wombats. I drew myself up, I assumed as much dignity as my dusty playsuit permitted, I used my fanciest vocabulary, I pretended I was terribly smart, I dropped a few names, I was boastful, I lied. Making sure they could see my notebook, I told them I was gathering material for magazine articles and the C.B.C. I even suggested that I might write a book about Cape Breton.

As I talked their faces changed; they began to look polite, then interested, almost eager. One of them said, "Girls, couldn't we make room in the car for Miss . . . ?" she smiled expectantly at me.

"Yes, do come with us," invited the blonde, opening the door of the back seat.

"Thank you very much but I don't want to crowd you. I'd much rather ride in the truck." Saying that made me feel good. As I walked away from the women I was overwhelmed with loyalty and gratefulness to the men who had been kind to me. Nothing could make me desert them now. What if I didn't reach Cheticamp? I could enjoy the adventure of trying to get there. I might even have fun! The man who was driving the women had loaned the boys a pump and the tire was blown up. We were ready to go on.

Because I'd been so nervous I had paid no attention at all to my benefactors except urbane little M. Ducette. Now I noticed that Norman, the driver, was almost handsome, with curly brown hair and a merry laugh. He told me that he was a student stationed at a research post on the north coast and had come from Windsor, Ontario. Don, a native, was tall, with an earnest face, deep blue eyes and the awkwardness of a person wearing his Sunday navy serge. "You're no doubt thinking me fretful about the truck," he said, "but I'd feel bad if anything happened to what belongs to the Co-op." In great detail he told me about the Co-operative Societies of Nova Scotia. Being manager of the Co-op store in Bay St. Lawrence, he is a staunch supporter of the system and thinks it is the answer to good government, offering the competition of capitalism and the profit-sharing of socialism. As I listened to him I was also carrying on a sporadic conversation with Norman about jazz bands and Cape Breton.

At three o'clock we reached Pleasant Bay where the blacksmith blew out the clogged gas line that had made the truck behave so badly. While we drank at a spring beside the road, M. Ducette said, "Are we not also in need of food? Let us go to the Timmis Lodge."

"They won't give us a meal at this hour," Norman was certain.

"Dey will, dey will," the little Frenchman held up a finger and rolled his eyes, "if you allow me to persuade the ladee in the kitchen."

From the lodge the view of the Bay was a perfect thing: masses of spray-splashed rock formed its deeply rounded curve; on the open shore fishing stages clustered round a dock; a gravel road wavered near the edge to a higher level where a steepled church gleamed white against the evergreen darkness of the mountain ridge; completing the semi-circle of land around the inlet, a purple promontory stretched to the horizon. Norm and I looked long and silently until he said, "That's what I mean, Edna, I go home and tell my family this country's got something but there's no way of making them understand it."

Don came up to us, "You like it?" he asked eagerly.

Norman made a speech: "With majesty like that to live with, Cape Bretonners couldn't miss having the character you're always yakking about."

The road between Pleasant Bay and Cheticamp is the most excitingly beautiful one that I have ever seen. It goes up and down the mountains, curves spirally round them, plunges deeply into the valleys, twists sharply at the narrow bridges that cross glinting streams, and almost all the time keeps within sight of the blue and shining sea. As we wound slowly round the timbered slopes of Mackenzie and French Mountains to a height of fourteen hundred feet, we could see miles of jagged shore where great crags had broken from the cliffs and tumbled into the triumphing ocean.

As the old truck joggled us along Norm concentrated on the driving. I exulted in the scenery and listened to Don, who wants to become an educated man by reading books chosen for him by his brother, a priest in Cheticamp. He told me he wants a good life in the Hereafter and is trying to prepare himself for it by being a good Catholic now. "But my brother says a good Catholic must be married," Don's long face was gloomy, "I've looked and looked but I canna find the right girl. There are so few hereabout to choose from and all they think of is Times. If I talk to them about books and politics they think me daft. The truth is I don't know how to approach them."

"Don't let him convert you to anything," Norm said to me, laughing.

The other man went on, " 'tis a serious thing to me, and often I dream of the girl: she'd have to be anxious for learning, of good character, and a little bit saving, a pretty face would be nice but not the most important." Don's body slumped beside me. "I don't think there is such a one."

We reached Cheticamp in the late afternoon. It stretched out long and narrowly on the strip of flat land that lay between the mountains and the sea. Along the main street modest shops and houses bordered the thoroughfare. Rising like a colossus in the centre of the lowly little town was the Roman Catholic Church with its attendant buildings and landscaped grounds. "The finest and largest church east of Quebec," Don told us proudly, "made of freestone from Cheticamp Island out there," he pointed.

Norm stopped at a service station to have our bad tire changed while he was going about his business of buying liquor for his boss. Don intended calling on his brother, the priest. M. Ducette was going home. And I? M. Ducette thought I should stay overnight in the town; the boys wanted me to return with them, assuring me that with the truck fixed they'd have me at the Harbour soon after nightfall. We arranged to meet in an hour at the Co-op store where I would tell them my plans.

63

M. Ducette continued to be my host. He took me first to the Inn where we were told they had already turned away several people and it was useless to try to find accommodation anywhere. "Then you shall come home with me to my old woman," declared my protector, whose farm is five miles south of the town. He told me his son was once in Ontario and people had been so kind to him that he would be happy only if he could return hospitality to someone from that province. I appreciated his generosity but wasn't sure his wife would share his sentiment. Also it had taken me so long to get to Cheticamp – fifty-eight miles in seven and three-quarter hours – that I decided I shouldn't refuse a way of getting out of it.

There was little time to see the mats that had lured me to make the trip. M. Ducette hurried me down the road to a tiny shop where he introduced me to the proprietress with the flourish of one who presents the wife of an American millionaire. Because it was the end of the season the stock of mats was low. I bought only a thirteen-inch square. My sponsor looked disappointed, the woman disgruntled. I explained that when I travelled home I couldn't carry a larger one with all my luggage and two swordfish swords. M. Ducette agreed so skeptically that I bought a dozen oranges for him to take home to his wife.

As we walked back to the Co-op store, M. Ducette mused, "I don't like to think of you leaving Cheticamp dis night in dat no-good truck. It is not to be trust, you may have to sleep in de mountains where dere are bear and deers and fox."

"I'm not afraid of animals," I said.

M. Ducette looked at me from the corners of his eyes, "And the young men?" he asked.

"They seem very nice."

He agreed warmly. "Dey are young men excellent, from dem you 'ave nothing to fear." He lowered his head and peered at me sagely under his sparce little eyebrows. "Besides, I think you are one who know it is always de woman who holds de key."

I thanked him for his confidence. He beamed happily then suddenly stiffened as a cat does when it sights a dog. "I cross de road," he muttered. I followed him to the other side where he walked quickly on the path, not speaking, his eyes straight ahead as if I didn't exist. I hurried to keep up with him, not liking to ask but wondering what had happened to the chummy little man who had been so attentive a moment before.

After we'd gone perhaps a hundred steps he turned his head cautiously towards the way we had come. A relieved sigh brought back his habitual smile. "Now we go again togedder."

I was puzzled.

"You see dat people dat pass us over dere?"

"Those three men?" I asked looking round.

"Dat fat pig in de middle wit' black glasses. He knows me and if he see me walking in Cheticamp with pretty young girl he will tell my wife and she will give me hell."

I said goodbye reluctantly to M. Ducette when the truck picked me up. Don and Norman were hungry again and so was I. We were told that Johnnie-on-the-Spot would not turn us a-way.

Johnnie's hotel was well used and not modern. Johnnie himself was sparkling, volatile, French. He greeted us in the lobby as if he had always known us. When we asked him for food he started in a quiet confidential tone, "Now you see dis is how it is: I have no fish. I can't get none, I have tried but dey are not catched." His voice kept rising. "If dey are not catched what can I do?" He raised his shoulders, looking utterly perplexed.

Norm said, "That's all right, we don't want fish."

"But dis is Tuesday and I am suppose to give fish." Johnnie was emphatic. "Church law make me do dis. But de fish do not know law, dey stay on de bottom. What can I do when fishes act dis way?"

We were nonplussed; we were starving.

Then Johnnie had a look of triumph, his eyes gleamed as they darted from one face to another. He almost whispered, "I have some steak, beautiful steak, thick and red it is, from a most gentille cow. I have know de cow dat is dis steak, docile, tendre," he rolled his eyes. "My Madeleine could cook him queeck with perhaps a little onion, you like steak with a leetle onion?" he tantalized. We were drooling.

Johnnie suddenly looked indifferent, he shrugged, he took steps towards the door. "The law say eat no meat dis Tuesday, I mus' go buy heggs from Mme. Bouchard." He walked into the street.

Norm ran after him. "We want that steak," he shouted.

Quickly Johnnie put his finger over his lips; he came back smiling, "Ladee, gentlemen," he said, "you are right, it is perhaps senseless to 'ave dis fine steak and let him spoil in dis warm day, n'est-ce pas? If you want him I will give him." Norm and I pounced on it when it was served, but being a fast day for Don he had to have eggs.

The truck, reloaded, refueled, retired, was eager to climb the mountains. All Don's attention was given to the driving. Norm, very gay, a little bit reckless, put his arm along the back of the seat because he liked the feel of my hair blowing against it, he said. "You know there's nothing feminine at the radar station."

"Why don't you come to Neil's Harbour and go out with a girl? Maggie Patterson would be nice."

"I value my life more than that, I've been told if a man comes in from outside the village boys gang up and run him out."

Before we reached the first curve on French Mountain the water in the radiator was boiling. We stopped at a spring where a dull black sedan was filling up too. Soon we had to stop again. Don found a rusty can and a trickle of water beside the road; Norm strained the water into the radiator through his handkerchief. The sedan struggled past us. Half way up the next hill it was stalled in the middle of the road. Despite the strain on the ailing truck, Don shoved the little car to the top and it ran down the other side and part way up the next rise. The truck pushed it over. By now daylight was gone. A soft yellow glow came from our headlights. The truck feebly helped the car into the darkness. Then we had a flat tire.

Norman was delighted; he was sure we'd have to spend the night on the mountain. Don, as he fumbled for tools, was very unhappy with the prospect. I wasn't worried at all: the night was warm, stars were shining, the boys were good company, they treated me like a princess; it was great to be with them, to know that one could meet such fine people on the road, that they were in the world at all.

The spare tire went on easily. We ran round a curve where the black sedan was waiting. Its people got out and came back to us for conference. Someone knew that the next incline was Mackenzie Mountain and the chugging old truck couldn't possibly shove the car over it; the two women, terrified of the night, asked if they and one of their three men might come with us. They climbed into the seat with Norman and me, the man rode in the back with Don. The truck hissed and spat, grumbled and growled, but kept going till we reached the Lodge at Pleasant Bay.

Mr. Timmis came out to greet us. While the women and the man from the black sedan followed him to a cabin where they were to sleep, Don said, "I think we'd better get some Gillet's lye to flush out our radiator."

"To hell with the radiator," Norm shouted, "we'll stay here over night. No more mountain climbing for me in that bastard truck. With her dim lights and lousy brakes we're liable to go over the edge and nobody'd find us till the leaves fall off the trees."

"That's what happened to some Americans last year," Mr. Timmis said as he joined us.

"Edna must stay, but I got to risk it," Don said, "my mother and sisters would worry till I got home."

"Better let 'em worry over you for a night than have 'em grieving over your body," Mr. Timmis reasoned.

"They'll think we stayed in Cheticamp for a night on the town," Norm suggested.

"They'd never think that of me," said Don, dolefully shaking his head.

"Right you are, ye stubborn Scotchman," Norm knew he was beaten. He put his arm around me. "Well, kid, I guess this is goodbye, and maybe forever. Better give us a kiss." His smack was resounding.

I turned to Don. But he said, "I don't think it's fitten for a girl to be kissin' a man unless they're married or promised, so if it's all the same to you, we'll just be shaking hands."

CHAPTER SEVEN

WE THINKS MIGHT BE HER'S IGERANT

WEDNESDAY, AUGUST 15

A family of tourists brought me back to Neil's Harbour before noon. We stopped on the way to watch a doe and her fawn in the woods, to drink at a stream where we saw the swift shadows of trout. We examined a stone replica of the huts used by crofters tending sheep in the Scottish hills – "the lone shieling of the misty island where still the blood is strong, the heart is Highland, and we in dreams behold the Hebrides." We admired the Big Intervale and the grandeur of Sunrise Valley. The tourists spoke about their motor trip, I talked about my fishing village at whose sight I had the feeling of coming home.

There is nothing to do this afternoon: the water is grey as the cloudy sky, gulls fly over the land – a sign of storm – a snapper boat bound for the safety of Dingwall harbour rises and falls behind the waves. Men sit idly in lee of the stages; women walk with arms and fingers modestly straightened against their thighs as skirts cling and billow; children, like leaves blown across a common, run quickly along with the wind; chickens resent their ruffled feathers erected like fan-shaped sails; cows lie unperturbed by fences, flicking flies with switchbroom tails.

I've slept a little while, I've written letters, I've walked on the stones along the shore. Broken shells, pieces of rope, bits of driftwood, bones of fish, the sole of a little child's shoe have told me that life is full of impressions: things I know someone would love bring a fleeting thought of friends who are far away; often the thought lingers lovingly, poignantly, it does not make me sad, there is no conflict, I am secure in knowing I have friends.

"Always writin', ain't you?" Henry Rider, carrying an empty bucket, sat beside me. "Must be someone you's awful fond of gettin' all them letters."

"Don't you write to your family in Newfoundland?"

"No, I never writes 'em, all that matters is I'm alive, if I ain't they'd hear soon enough. I'm not much of a hand fer writin', never know what to say and 'tain't easy for me to put it down. I don't know how you doos it so fast. I guess you must a got a lot o' schooling, haven't you?"

"I suppose so."

"That's what I figgered. I says to men, 'That girl's eddicated,' I says, 'her's always writin', we thinks might be her's igerant 'cause 'er don't know nothin' about what we got round 'ere and is always askin' how we doos things and what's they for but that's best way for gettin' eddicated,' I says." Henry cut off a wad of tobacco and shoved it inside his cheek.

"Ain't like one feller I knowed had a lot o' schoolin'; nice feller 'e were too, lived in Rose Blanche in summer time, and d'you know what 'e done? He'd get used up old stamps and stick 'em down into a book. Yes, dear, ye never seen anythin' so foolish like as that man, full growed, sittin' there stickin' them stamps and lookin' at 'em like they was a fortune 'e'd got hold of. One day I tooked he a packet o' letters I found in old strongbox o' me grandf'er. Well say, I thought 'e were takin' a fit when 'e seen 'em, and when 'e stopped ravin', 'e took wallet out o' britch pocket and hands me a five dollar bill. But I give it back, I wouldn't take money for no used up ol' stamps ain't no good for nobody." Henry stiffly got to his feet and picked up his pail. "I got t' go now and fill this drat bucket for Hattie Buffet. See you around."

Most of the brooks, as the wells of the village are called, have been dried up for some time. The people at the top of the hill were the first to start carrying water about a mile from the spring behind the preacher's house. Now those living at road level are carrying too. The water in the Malcolms' well is very low: instead of the dipper, there is now a cup beside the pail in the bathroom.

The best place to bathe is in the Pond formed by a stream whose mouth is blocked by a strip of beach, making a pool with water warmer and calmer than the North Atlantic except when the sea is wild enough to break through the sand bar and mingle its salt water with the fresh. It is glorious for swimming, with firm white sand on its floor – and so well secluded that I can take off my suit in the water and have a bath with Miss Katie's pink soap.

That is what I was doing this afternoon when clumsy big Max crashed down the steep path to the beach. I was still as a fish in the water and he didn't know I was there; he came up to my things on the stones, gave them a quick going over, picked up a slipper, dropped it then crossed the sand and looked at the sea. He came back to my coat and stood over it, head inquiringly on one side. I splashed my hand in the water. He saw me then, wagged his great tail and barked.

I've discovered a perfect place from which to watch the sunset; the top of a fence isn't cosy but after boards and rock and bumpy ground the surface of a rail is merely a different shape to be impressed on my posterior. Half way between Alec's house and Mrs. Pride's I can look at the rosy light on the fishing boats in the bay, I can tell if there is activity on the dock, turning my head I can watch anyone who comes along the main road and the lane that winds up to the houses on the hill. I am like a decoy; everyone who passes can see me and come to talk to me if they will – and I hope they will.

I hadn't been sitting long tonight when a fisherman came a-long: "Hain't gone yet, I see. Must loike this place."

"It's so different from what I'm used to: I'm liking it more every day."

"I guess it were some strange for you at first." He leaned a-gainst the fence beside me, looking at the bay. A man with a gentle face, blue eyes and sandy hair showing round the back of his swordfishing cap, he is the man who gave me the sword on the night I came to the Harbour. His name – Miss Laurie told me – is Matt Clipper. He turned to me with a grin: "I guess you thinks we talks funny round 'ere, eh? We calls everything 'e and we says bean 'stead of bin, and heyess for eyes. Hit's 'ard on young uns goin' to school, teacher learns 'em one thing and they comes 'ome and we says something helse and they don't know which be roight. I tells mine teacher knows best and they gotta teach we." Matt Clipper's voice was soft and slow, I longed to put down every word he said, but no writing could reproduce the heart-warming way he said it.

"When you first come we says, 'That one don't come from Up-per Canada, must come from States.'"

"What made you think that?"

"Them from hinland be always findin' things wrong with we, always tellin' us what they got better at home, loike we didn't 'ave nothin'. Americans seems to think Harbour's roight good." He took out a pocket knife and opened it. "We had a couple stay to our house one year, wouldn't moind seein' 'em come back. After they left they wrote a letter and sent things to the children at Christmas – dolls 'n that." He took a slice off the fence rail. "We don't git tourists 'ere 'cause there's no room for 'em, sea-son's too short for us to spend money fixin' up places." He cut another shaving. "You never can tell about people neither," he said. "During war a man and 'is woman come round 'ere in car. I said they was Germans and told Alec but 'e says, 'Oh no, they's much too friendly, couldn't be Germans.' Well say, they had cam-eras and they walked round all over this here and snapped and snapped. They got men to take 'em out in boats and asked 'em to go near shore. What's more, they kep' drawin' maps, we ketched 'em at it, maps of whole shore round 'ere they had. I knowed they was Germans and sure as hell when they went to

Sydney they was nabbed."

Matt whittled a few slices. "Lots 'o people comes round 'ere in summer and wants rides in boats; some even offers to pay fer it. They says 'Whoi don't you take tourists out instead o' fishin'? You'd make more money.' " Matt raised his head proudly. "We tells 'em we's fishermen, just loike they's lawyers, er doctors, er whatever they is. Fishin' is our job."

"Where I live people go fishing for fun."

Matt looked up from his whittling with a twinkle in his blue eyes. "Maybe you thinks we's lazy, layin' round stages loike we doos?"

"I have wondered that," I admitted.

"Fisherman's got to wait fer a cam," he said, "got to have toime fer settin' and mendin' 'is naits. When a man is fishin' 'e works terrible hard; 'e's got to make enough money in six months to last 'im all year. Soon as 'e's got it 'e can quit if 'e's moinded, no use workin' at fall fishin' if storehouse is filled and ye got money to do ye till spring; woife don't loike fer her man to be out on the water when it's woild and cold." Matt raised his cap and scratched his head with a finger. "You don't need a pile o' money round 'ere," he said, "not loike ye do where you's from. We doos everything for ourself that needs doin': builds our own housses, makes our own boats, fixes our engines; we go huntin', doos our own butcherin', cut and chop our wood," Matt snapped his knife shut. "So long as we got enough to keep us warm and full and droi, we don't need more, I always thinks if folks be koind and got their health, that's the most himportant."

Two little blonde girls with braids came up and pulled at Matt's hands, they wouldn't speak because I was there and they were shy but somehow he knew and told me they wanted him to help find the cow that had not come from the hills to be milked. Hand in hand, laughing and talking, they walked down the road towards the Trail – while I stayed on my fence rail with the glowing conviction that I had been given a glimpse of the heart of Neil's Harbour.

A long-faced fisherman came from the direction of the stages, rested his arms on a fence post beyond me, stared at the water, and very soon strolled away. Several people passed by me on the road. Then I saw Andrew Clipper, the lighthouse keeper, coming down the hill carrying his lantern and I slipped off my rail to follow him.

For me Neil's Harbour is dominated by the Light. No matter where I wander it is the focal point of all I see. When I sit on the fence to watch the fishing boats at sunset, the Light beams protectively down on them. When I look from my bedroom window at the cluster of stages I see the Light above them. From the beach I see the Light over the jetties across the bay. When I walk along the roads from the Cove or the Trail, I walk towards the Light. Everything in the village has a background of sea, rock or hill, but the Light rises against the sky. Built on the highest part of the Point near the edge towards the open sea, it stands aloof and alone, sturdily guiding and guarding. Its sloping white sides, its red metal cap with the balcony round it have style as they rise into the blue; it is modern, it is classic, it is beautiful; it is the symbol of security for all who live by the sea.

The keeper of the Light, a thick little dark man who looks like a Scottie, took me with him to watch him perform the most responsible job in the Harbour. He unlocked the lighthouse door, filled a can from one of the barrels of kerosene that stood in a small square room, then climbed the narrow stairway to the trapdoor entrance of the metal chamber that houses the Light. There he removed the duck curtains from the windows and polished the sparkling glass while I looked with wonder at the dim outline of St. Paul's Island beyond faraway Cape North, and Smokey Mountain twenty miles to the south.

Turning towards the Light I examined the heavy, prismatic magnifying glass supported by shining brass, which sends the rays of the two-wicked lamp into the darkness over the sea. "Everything looks so new and clean," I said, "how long has the Light been here?"

"It ain't new, miss," the keeper showed me the thickness of the paint, " 'twere built in 1893; but we keeps it careful and shining like 'cause lives might be lost if it ain't kep' good. Lots o' fine ships went down off this coast before the lights went up. But only one I knows of got wrecked off the Point since this light come on: the *Velundie,* a large vessel struck on the east side with nobody lost; that were in 1921 and she stayed on rocks till next year.

"The movin' pitcher *The Sea Raiders* was made 'ere because

they needed a wreck fer it. They took one o' their women – awful pretty lookin' she was, but painted – and dipped 'er in water and brought 'er in on a stretcher like she was drownded – we watched 'em doin' it – and they asked us to walk across the beach with our hand barrels o' fish and they took our pitchers in our oilskins just like we was workin' and some people that knowed us seen the pitcher in town and told us we looked right natural."

On my way down from the Lighthouse I saw Molly leaning in the doorway of her home. "What was you doin' at all day?" she called. "I thought moight be ye'd come round." Warmed by her greeting I sat on the stoop beside her. "My Gohd," she cried, looking past me, "half me washing's blowed away in the gale." I moved to retrieve it but she shrugged her shoulders, "Don't bother none, it'll come back." She smiled and nodded her head as diapers and dishtowels clung to the fence. "Lucky it never blowed in with the pig."

A miniature of Molly and a smaller solemn-eyed child with blonde curls and an alarmingly red face squeezed between us. "Gwendoline, take that lipstick from Frillie, there ain't nothin' left to it and last week it were that tall." She held apart her thumb and fingers, smiling her carefree smile.

"Frillie's an odd name, Molly, where did you git it?" I asked.

"Fred give it to 'er. Oi don't know where it come from, I think he made it oop," she grinned. "Noice though, ain't it?"

We sat for a while in silence as a schooner came into the bay to land a fish at the dock. The children ran down to watch it. "Aren't you afraid the little ones will fall in?" I asked Molly.

"Oh I goes down and looks now and again but roight now with all them men down there somebody'd fish 'em out quick enough. They couldn't be in more than a little whoile." Molly turned towards the main road. "Fred's drivin' Gladdie's car over to Dingwall tonight, takin' Clipper boys with." We saw the car go up the steep lane that wound around the houses. "Now if that ain't loike Fred," Molly said, "goin' way up there after the bastards. Whoi couldn't them come down that hill? Can hardly cloimb it with a car but Fred doos everything for anybody if they asks him to." There was pride and affection in Molly's voice. She sat down beside me. "Oi wonder where to they're goin' at over in Dingwall, must be boats in from Newfoundland with rum."

We didn't talk much after that but Molly kept smiling with a mysterious half impish twinkle as if she knew a wonderful secret. And I felt unaccountably as if I knew one too.

When Molly went to tuck her youngest in bed, I walked past the stages where the middle-sized boys were playing a game that might have been cricket if they'd had a ball and bat instead of a rusty tin can and a stick. The men sitting on the grass were encouraging them and there was a moment of excitement whenever someone hit the can and ran for a goal.

The long evenings at the Harbour are difficult for me. I don't know what to do with myself except to walk along the road to the Cove where people are always strolling; with its grassy banks and concealing spruces, it is the Road for romancing – unlike the open road from the Trail, which can be seen by everyone in the fishermen's houses on the hill.

It was nearly dark when three little girls came strolling. I said hello and they walked beside me without speaking. They were perhaps eleven years old with wispy blonde hair and flimsy cotton dresses. Not knowing what to talk about I unfortunately reminded them that school would start in a couple of weeks. They groaned. "But maybe it won't," one of them said, "Cove boys broked windows in schoolhouse and they ain't got glass to fix 'em."

"They ain't got no teachers yet neither," said another. "We needs two, there's over a hunnert to be teached."

"Won't the ones you had last year be back?"

"No, we has different teachers every year, they never comes back, does they, Ellen? They don't loike in winter when we's froze up, can't git out till spring, mail sometimes don't come for three weeks and they can't hear from their folks. Anyhow they say it's good to change 'em, then us don't git sassy with 'em loike we doos if we knows 'em too long."

"Last one we had were only seventeen year old. She were roight smart too."

"What will you do if you can't go to school?"

They giggled. "Help at home, scrub, wash dishes." Ellen lamented, "We got twelve into our house, Susan and Ada only got eight."

"Where do you belong?" Susan asked me.

I told them.

"Is Ontario far?" Ada, the little one, wondered.

"Roight far," Ellen answered. "D'you do much swordfishing there?"

As we approached the Hall we heard feet clattering on the outside platform where several young boys were shoving each other around. "Let's go down and tarment en," my little pals suggested. They ran down the slope and stood wistfully on the edge of the dance floor. The boys stood still and no one spoke. The little girls came back to me. "You must git awful lonesome here by yerself," Susan said.

"I do sometimes."

"You better stay with we," Ellen offered.

"Yes, stay with we," the small one echoed.

We walked back towards the village. Men and boys sitting high on the rocks at the side of the Road flashed a light on us. "Come on," Ellen said excitedly, "let's go oop." They climbed the rocks into the darkness and I walked on alone. In the wan light I saw movement at the sides of the Road. Several boys and girls passed me with their arms around each other, a few walking alone said good-evening; I heard men come up behind me.

"You look awful lonesome tonight," one said.

"Don't you want company?" asked another.

Farther along I heard a softly spoken, "Come with me, dear."

I walked faster. There was a restless feeling about the Road; a wondering and waiting and wanting – and a shyness, thank God.

CHAPTER EIGHT

CALVIN WILL TAKE YE CODFISHIN'

Thursday, August 16

When I heard the reedy crowing of young roosters this morning I considered dressing quickly and running down the shore to go out with the swordfishermen, but I was still in bed savouring the resinous fragrance of a spruce fire cooking the porridge when their boats left the collar.

The Harbour is a quiet waiting place when the men are on the sea. There is no one on the roads, the wharves are deserted. Alec doesn't bother to open his store till mid-morning, the women stay in their houses, little girls play with dolls on porches, little boys disappear on expeditions along the shore, old men sit beside the stages whittling and yarning away the hours.

As I crossed the stubbly common to the eastern side of the Point I felt an unreasoning resentment towards the fate – or the stubbornness in myself – that keeps me in this lonely place. I sat

77

near the hollowed bank where I could watch the boats weave back and forth in the blue of the sea and the birds fly high and free in the blue of the sky.

There was no wind; the Atlantic was serene and smooth as a piece of sparkling crystal, as calm as the artificial duck pond in Victoria Park at home.

But round massive formations of granite that stretched away from the land, the water eddied and swirled; over low worn rock it kept boiling, it splashed against jagged islets, showering their tips with spray. I could not understand it: there was no wildness on the sea, there were no waves, only myriad sparkles of sunlight glinting on infinite silver.

Mesmerized by its beauty, I kept watching, not really thinking, but idly, quietly, wondering, until somehow I knew that under the sea's peaceful surface there were tides coming and going, ebbing and flowing, powerful currents that roved through all the seas of the world – currents of infinite power.

The thought thrilled me. It overwhelmed me. It seemed the most marvellous knowledge, the heart of every secret, every mystery. I can't explain it. I can only say I felt rapture, secureness, sureness of something great, something boundless, eternal. That somehow it was part of me and I was part of it, part of the sea, of the sky, of the rocks, of the grass, even of the pesky fly that kept buzzing around me.

I stood up and stretched out my arms, I think that I shouted. I slid over the edge of the bank to the tumbled rocks below. From one battered slope to another I leapt till my face was wetted with spray. Then slowly I climbed to the common.

Molly's children found me near the stony beach. Nine-year-old Freddie carrying curly-headed little Frillie put her down beside me. Gwendoline sat across the road behind us because her dress was dirty and she didn't want me to see; Jeanie was collecting grass to make a bird's nest; Philip was throwing stones; Sandy, very shy, sat close to Freddie and didn't say a word. When Frillie toddled unsteadily from us Freddie said, "Careful now, dear, don't fall," picked her up and hugged her. "Poor darlin', Mummie didn't comb yer hair this mornin' did she?" He brushed her curls from her eyes. She squiggled to get away. "Quiet now, dear, don't be bad; give me kiss." Frillie ducked

78

her head like a little flirt. "Oh she's some bad," Freddie said and kissed her cheek.

Then Gwendoline stirred something in a wooden vat that released the concentrated essence of all the stenches in the world. Running away from it I asked what it was. Gwendoline running with me answered, "Hit's blubber for makin' hoil; they puts livers in barrel and lets sun melt en. Don't it stink awful?"

"Lots things stinks awful," said Philip, carefully avoiding a cow flap on the road as he ran with us towards the wharf.

One of the snapper boats was still tied up. "Aren't you going out this morning?" I asked a man huddled on a post.

"We is but we's waitin' fer the preacher, 'e wants to go swordfishin'."

"Doesn't he know you go out at seven?"

"'e knows, but preachers don't git up so early as fishermen doos."

"He's held you up for three hours."

"That's all right for the preacher," the man calmly spat tobacco juice into the water. He grinned, "Maybe he'll git us into heaven fer it."

Bustling along the road, swinging a brown paper lunch bag, the Anglican parson wore his clerical black and back-buttoned collar, shiny rubber boots and a swordfishing cap. "All right now, men," he said briskly, "let's get aboard."

Yesterday morning I asked the men on the wharf if they knew who might take me codfishing. "Calvin Leaf will take you," Big Jim Clipper was always teasing. "He's got a roight foine boat and lots o' room hinto it. 'e always goes out alone and 'e ketches more fish than anybody in Neil's Harbour." A round-faced man with a quarter-inch of stubble looked uneasy.

"I don't think he wants to take me," I said.

"Whoi sure 'e do, Calvin loves to take the ladies out in 'is boat, you know how bachelors is," Jim tittered. "You be on shore good and early, Calvin will be waitin' fer you." Poor old Calvin's weathered face was mahogany under his whiskers; he squirmed and walked away towards his rickety saw-mill.

This morning Calvin was splitting cod with the men on the dock – as usual. "Did you get a good catch?" I asked him, and he nodded.

"Yis sir," Jim Clipper said, "Calvin got the best ketch 'e's had all summer. Never were up and out so early in 'is loife, scared to death you'd be down ahead of 'im."

When I left the dock to go home for my dinner, Henry Rider walked along with me. "Ye really want to go codfishin', don't ye?"

"I really do."

"I'll take ye this evening if it's fine."

"Wonderful! I'll be ready," I said, and was suddenly aware of unsteadiness in my middle.

For three hours now I've been lying on my bed. I've tried to read *War and Peace* but the book is too heavy to hold. I've counted the hundred and forty-six narrow boards that make the walls and sloping ceiling of my little room. I've stared at the pictures: a dateless calendar on which King George V and Queen Mary, very faded, look uncomfortably noble; a black tapestry with camels and Arabs standing round a well like mourners gazing at a corpse; a page of flowers from a seed catalogue and a framed Jesus, in sepia, leaning against a rock and praying.

I have a fever, I think I'm quite sick. The doctor is vacationing and everyone along sixty miles of coast is supposed to stay healthy till he comes back. The biggest house on the Cove Road, a Red Cross Hospital with seven beds and a room for delivering babies, is closed for a week. I wonder what they'd do if I died here? Send me out on the *Aspy*, I suppose – or on the fish boat.

For supper tonight Katie gave me an anaemic milk pudding and Flakey Pilot biscuits with a hard-tack nautical look and absolutely no taste. After eating I sat on the couch in the kitchen, stroking the moth-eaten cat and listening to the little old woman. She was frightened. She said someone gets into the house and sleeps in her bed: first it was a man but later it was a girl who had run away to get married. "It's terrible when people leave the house and you don't know how they got out, unless they went through the top." She eyed the ceiling timidly.

Katie smiled at her pityingly, "You'd better go to bed, Mother."

"I'm afraid to, somebody might come in. It's awful when you

don't feel safe." She crossed her arms tightly across her chest and looked around with fear-filled eyes. Miss Laurie sat in front of her and took her hand. "You're safe, dear, we're all here with you."

"It doesn't matter, they'll get in anyway."

Miss Laurie shook her head and said, "You have a dimple in your chin, Mother." The wrinkled old woman smiled, "That's a sign of beauty."

I went out to tell Henry I couldn't possibly go fishing but he wasn't anywhere around.

Tired and ill, I huddled on the edge of the sea while daylight was leaving the world; misery in my mind and loneliness in my heart, a solid lump I seemed, like the rocks that lay around me. I did not long for home, friends, comfort, I wanted only great white wings to swoop and soar with the birds, to take me sound and free, away and away and away.

With her little children playing around her, Molly sat on the cribbing of an old dock. I sat wearily beside her. We didn't talk much, we looked at the clouds in the darkening sky. Molly pulled her gum out of her mouth and folded it in again; sometimes she cracked it. Philip called, "Molly, here comes Lizzie Deaver."

"Whoi so she do," Molly greeted her friend with pleasure. Lizzie, a stout young woman with a top front tooth missing, shy at first because of me, kept covering her mouth with her hand. But soon she talked about going places. "I'd like to go to England," she said.

"Would you?" Molly was surprised. "It's awful far."

"I know, but I'd like to see where they have the Queen."

"Yes, 'twould be good to see that," Molly nodded.

"I might go down to Sydney this fall," Lizzie said, "does you good to git away."

"Yes, it doos," Molly agreed, "some toime Oi'd loike to leave keeds behind and go away for a whole week."

"Where to?" I asked.

Molly's eyes were full of dreams, "Oi'd loike to go to Ingonish and stay at the Keltic Lodge where the Goverman General was to."

Lizzie gasped, "Oh Molly, not with all them swells?"

"Whoi not?" Molly pulled out her gum. "They's only people, pisses same as we."

"Yes, but they pays twenty dollars a day just for what they eats," Lizzie said.

"Moi Gohd, ye'd have to eat a lot to git twenty dollars worth into ye, wouldn't you now? What could they feed 'em would be worth twenty dollars?"

"Ain't got nothin' there we ain't got here, has they?" Lizzie asked.

Molly said, "Holy jumpin' Cheesus, Oi'd loike to go and foind out."

CHAPTER NINE

JUST LOOK AT ALL DEM ROCKS

FRIDAY, AUGUST 17

Since I've been here on my own I've felt independent and happy most of the time but having dysentery isn't any fun. I want someone to be kind to me and dammit, Miss Katie talks gruffly and keeps looking at me with the same cold glare that the chickens in the front yard give me when I pass them. Actually I think she's upset, I think she's afraid I might become terribly ill and she'd have me on her hands. And what could she do with me?

Her mother said, "People who have what you've got should go out and live in the bush till they're better."

Miss Laurie watches me anxiously. This morning she brought out a large black bottle of Pain Killer whose label guarantees a cure for a long list of ailments in both man and beast. To please her I took a spoonful. WOWOWOWOWOWOW! I'd like to see its effects on a boa constrictor. I should soon be dead or cured.

Meanwhile I'm lying in the shade of the lighthouse where occasionally I see Tommy Seaforth's head popping round a corner of the nearest stage. Tommy has a look of quality, an Eton-collar choir-boy look, shining white teeth that protrude slightly, and curly hair that matches his warm brown eyes. I catch glimpses of him wherever I go; I think he follows me. When our eyes meet, he smiles then disappears; if I speak to him he blushes and runs away. About the same age – twelve, I think – is Kennie Candle (Kendall) whose sweetness attracted me on the dock the first night; he doen't follow me but I see him often looking at me curiously before his face lights with its heavenly smile.

To these youngsters I suppose I am from the glamorous, far-away world they dream about: a world with hockey teams, airplanes, racing cars, telephones and neon lights. I wonder how they imagine it? They've never been farther than Dingwall, which is no larger than Neil's Harbour.

When I dreamed of the sea in Ontario, it was of towering waves, great rocks and fishing; I didn't think at all about people! Now while I am living my dream of a rockbound coast, I look at Tommy and Kennie, at all the people of the Harbour in their wild, beautiful world so unlike that to which I am accustomed, and I am overwhelmed by their strangeness; at times I say to myself with unbelieving wonder: "These are part of my country; Neil's Harbour is Canada!"

Being alone, I was afraid to be friendly when I arrived here. Everyone was so different that I didn't know what to say. Now I tell myself: "They are people, they eat and sleep and wear clothes and are afraid and lonely and angry and shy and curious just like me." If I keep remembering that, I seem to understand them; if I look at them and listen to them, if I am completely absorbed and aware of them, I feel natural and happy and free, and they laugh with me and accept me and I am fond of them.

Molly found me on the Point. She wanted to show me the little pools amongst the rocks where it is safe to strip and bathe in the sun-warmed water. "Ain't them grand?" she exclaimed. "Don't need bathtub in house when ye got those. Even the old maid comes here for bath, you watch if she don't; Gohd wouldn't Oi loike to supprise 'er some day when 'er's mother naked. But I'll bet she don't take off 'er big straw hat, moight git a freckle."

Molly squatted to pick black shoebutton berries and pop some into her mouth. "Droi and seedy, but sweet – crowberries we calls 'em. Don't plants feel noice and springgy under yer feet?" She looked at me impishly. "Loike to lay in 'em, wouldn't you?" She wriggled her flat little body in its red print dress.

A hen squawked suddenly amongst the thick low bushes. "Jest listen to the slut," Molly said. "Gone and laid an egg; she knows I'll never foind it; they always walks far away from 'em before they starts cacklin' loike that. Shoo, Shoo!" Molly tossed a pebble at the hen. "The sons o' bitches always lays away if I don't bar 'em up."

"Where do you look for the eggs?"

"Oh usually under things loike that old mattress down there on the beach; they's awful hard to foind, can't never tell where they'll put 'em; then when they gits broody they goes and sets on 'em."

We stopped to pick up bits of shell. Molly said, "Them's mussels, roast 'em in oven and shells falls off; there's good meat inside, got to pick it out with pin. Can do same with snails." She examined a shell. "Snails be funny little boogers, ain't they? No harm to 'em but you be careful when you's swimming that you don't step on a whoore's egg, they sea urchins is full o' prickles will give you a fester."

We walked to the hollowed edge of the Point to watch the swirling tide. "Gosh, Molly, you're lucky to live by all this." Molly nodded and smiled her mysterious smile. "Yis, wouldn't loike to live away from the wahter." Her eyes shone. "Should see this when there's storm, that's grandest of all, ye can't git out on Point, water washes acrost the road and clean over the Light."

When Molly left me to do her daily laundry, I watched the fish boat leave. I suppose I should be on it, my week here is up, but I couldn't travel to Sydney while I am sick; besides, Molly has shown me there is unexplored treasure at Neil's Harbour.

Miss Katie, wearing her big straw sun hat, came to the dock with a tin plate to get fish for our dinner. "You'd better get out of the sun and lie down or you'll be sicker than ever," she warned me.

I shuffled meekly out of her sight, returning to the dock when she'd left it. Henry was there. "Where was you to last evening?" he asked me.

"I came to tell you I couldn't go fishing but you weren't around."

"I were waiting for you till two o'clock then I went up to stage and mended me nait. Won't be free to take ye atall now, me wife's comin' on *Aspy* today," he said and walked glumly away.

"I'm sure he said he'd take me in the evening," I spoke to a fisherman who had heard our conversation. "I was here right after supper.

"You was too late," the fisherman said, "evening is after noon. We gits up at three-four o'clock in marnin' for fishin', by ten we's back, splits our fish and is awful hungry for dinner at noon; then is evening and we works or sets around shore till supper time; then is night and we goes to bed."

The earth in Neil's Harbour is too shallow to support much vegetation but in a corner of their front yard the Malcolms have planted potatoes. While I lay on my bed after dinner Miss Laurie was bending over the plants and knocking potato bugs into a can. When she crossed the yard to the cow barn Katie called, "Laurie, you forgot to close the garden gate," and hurried to shut out vigilant marauders – white, mottled grey, auburn and black, the chickens are curious, cautious, greedy, always alert for movement in their domain.

Sometimes the big white rooster comes up on the steps to the kitchen door, his red comb flopping as he turns to look arrogantly at his motley harem and proclaim his superiority with a long loud rr-rr-rrooooooooooooooooooo! The women in the house show a mild excitement as they delightedly remark, "The white rooster's crowing on the steps again!"

"That's a certain sign that we'll have company," they've explained to me several times.

"Does it never fail?"

"I don't think so, someone always comes, though it may be only Charlotte Clipper fetching milk."

When I heard the whistle of the *Aspy* I dragged myself down to the wharf where I stood alone to watch the unloading. Henry, burdened by bags, boxes, a large woman and several half-grown children, passed by me without a sign.

86

A man I had not seen before came up to me. Not old, not young, he had a nose that would have made a cartoonist whip out a pencil; it was a long flat nose, drooping and spreading so prominently one realized with surprise that above it was a pair of bleary eyes and beside it were cheeks with deep creases. This comic creature obsequiously touched his limp tweed cap and came close enough for me to smell his beery breath. At the same time I was aware that villagers standing near were watching us and expecting something to laugh at. "You are the artist, ain't you?" he asked me. "I heard you're making pictures."

"I just try to draw some of the things I like around here. I'm not good at it."

"Well I got something I want to show you." He fumbled with the pocket of his windbreaker and brought out a flat little packet. Pulling open the string he unwrapped the brown paper and from between two pieces of cardboard produced a snapshot which he handed me with shaking fingers. It was a worn, over-exposed picture of two men standing in front of a shack in the woods with snow half way to their knees. "That's me," he said proudly, pointing at one of the tiny figures whose features were almost undiscernible.

"It's very nice," I said to please him.

"It's the only picture I ever had took, I'd like to have it drawed bigger so I could hang it on the wall. When I heard an artist was staying in town I thought I'd see if you could do it for me." He looked fondly at the picture. "That was the happiest day of my life. I was out cutting wood with men from Neil's Harbour; being's I'm not a fisherman they make out I'm different from other folk and leave me near always alone but that day in the bush I was like all the rest." Looking at his serious, homely face as he wrapped up his precious picture, I knew I would never see beauty that would make me more sorry I am not an artist.

There is so little to do after supper in Neil's Harbour that, despite my disability, I didn't want to miss the sale of women's work tonight with food and dancing after. By the time I found enough energy to reach the Hall, everything had been sold but a satin blouse and a child's jumper.

People were chatting in little groups round the outdoor platform when a pleasant-faced young man asked me to dance a square. I told him I was about to go home. He said, "To tell ye de trut', miss, I was thinking of doing the same. I wouldn't mind walking along wit' you."

As we started down the road together I heard little girl voices call, "He's married, Aidna."

He told me his name is Danny McCovan and he works in the coal mine that runs under the sea at Sydney Mines. I've always wondered about miners: why a man would work underground when there are so many things he could do to make a living in the sun. Danny said, "I don't mean no disrespect, miss, but if you wouldn't mind sitting down I'd like to tell you." We perched on two rocks between the road and the sea where Harbour sheep were grazing. "Me fadder was killed in de mine a few years ago – burned he was – and I thought then I'd like a change. I went clear across country as far as Vancouver, I worked on all kinds o' jobs, in factories, on farms, on docks; I was gone a couple years but I couldn't stick it, I come back to de mine."

"Do you like it that well?"

"It's all right; the dust is healthy for your lungs, they say, we get fair pay and we don't work such long hours no more. Dey're even giving us holidays now. I thought I'd spend my week in Neil's Harbour wit' my mother's sister but I'm going home to-morrow on the bus, I can't stick it here."

"Don't you like it?"

"Gahd no, dis ain't no place to live." He bent towards me. "To tell you de trut', miss, I got a little place o' my own at Sydney Mines, dere is a paved road in front and de bus passes every half hour. I got a bit o' garden and some pretty flowers, you should see the petunias I got dis year; pink, white, and purple, right solid. I'll bet you ain't seen a petunia since you come to dis place, have you?"

"Now that you mention it, I don't think I've seen any flowers at all."

"Of course you ain't. De trouble wit' dis place is de people don't care enough. Dey're too lazy to do anything. Now if dey'd git some dynamite and blow out dem dere rocks at de side o' de road and plant flowers dey'd have it really nice."

"But they could never get rid of the rocks."

88

Danny shook his head, "Dat's de trouble, dey got too many. Just look at all dem rocks, all over de place, and at de Cove it's even worse. At Sydney Mines we got good flat land wit' stuff growin' nice, none o' de wild look dis place got." He leaned towards me, "What I can't figger is why a girl like you stays here when you don't have to."

"It interests me, it's so different from anything I've ever known."

"It sure is different, I never seen anything like it nowheres. And the people's different too. Did you ever see such carrying on as dere is on dis here road at night? The fellows don't know how to act, dey run off wit' one girl, den leave 'er and try anodder – acting silly like dey don't know notting." Danny lowered his voice impressively. "Night before last when you walked past dat gang beside de road I was behind you and I heard what happened."

"Oh they always whistle like that and say, 'Hello dear,' they call everybody dear, the children do when they're playing, and the grown-ups the same. I guess it's a friendly Newfoundland custom."

Danny looked at me speculatively, "You like it, eh?" Then quick as a mink he got off his rock and tried to kiss me. I stood up. "I don't mean no disrespect, miss, I just thought it would be kind of nice." And Danny tried again.

I found the road in the moonlight. Danny didn't follow me; he called out, "What's de matter, is my breath bad or something?"

CHAPTER TEN

IT'S THE CATALOGUES THAT'S CAUSIN'
ALL THE TROUBLE IN THE WORLD

SATURDAY, AUGUST 18

"I'll give you no breakfast this morning till you've bought yourself a dose of castor oil," Katie said sharply when I came downstairs.

I crossed over to Alec's store but couldn't make myself ask for
the obvious remedy in front of the row of men who sat with legs
dangling from the edge of the platform. I was hungry, I was
weak, the scales on the dock showed yesterday that I have lost
five pounds.

Seeking sympathy, I went up the road to Alec's wife. "Laws,
girl, you do look washed out," she exclaimed, "have you been
drinking water?"

"Lots of it."

"That's it then! Doctor told me before he left it wasn't fit to drink with the brooks so low. I'll give you some strawberry extract I always give the children when they've got summer complaint."

I swallowed a spoonful of healing syrup and felt better almost immediately. "Now I'll go home and see if Katie will give me some breakfast."

"Wouldn't she give it you?" Elsa laughed. "Katie scolds but she means well. That's her way." Elsa poured two cups of coffee from the pot on the stove and made me a piece of toast. "Katie is an unhappy woman; she had a good job in Boston, belonged to clubs and had lots of friends, then her mother got sick and she gave it all up to come home and help. Laurie didn't ask her to, mind you, still she couldn't manage the old lady alone with the cow and the chickens." Elsa sipped her coffee. "Katie's been back six years now but she don't seem to belong no more, though she grew up here." Elsa looked to see that little Marie was safe in the yard. "And the worst of it is that the sacrifice Katie is making brings no satisfaction. The old lady don't know her no more than if she was a dark stranger; she keeps complaining about the foreigner that does the work in the house and wants Laurie to send her away." Elsa's sweet face was earnest. "You can imagine how that hurts Katie. You might say she has given up her life for the old lady – of course Mrs. Malcolm is sick in the head and don't know any better."

Finding a place to sit outdoors takes up much of my time; shade, shelter from wind, and a not uncomfortable base rarely come together in the Harbour. A spot that is almost perfect at one time is unbearable at another. The wind has a knack of whirling round walls, of finding little hollows below a bank or behind a rock. Buildings create the only shade: but the warehouses on the Point are set on stones that defy human contours, there are too many chickens round the houses, the sunburnt field near the Lighthouse is crisp and prickly, the luscious patch of grass behind Alec's store is the stamping ground of vagrant horses, the tempting green between the stages is strictly fishermen's preserve.

In a niche that is only partially exposed at the moment, I have been writing letters to my friends and family. I haven't asked to have my mail forwarded from Halifax because each day might be my last one here; my hitch-hiking at the beginning of the week and my complaint at the end of it have detained me – I tell them and myself –though actually I'm glad I've had such good excuses to stay longer.

It seems fairly crazy but I've noticed that it is only when I've been lonely or especially happy and pleased with the Harbour that I am restless and want to leave it. I want to talk about it. I want to tell people how beautiful and real it is.

Somehow there is excitement in its monotony. Though nothing happens, each day brings wonder and a new delight. There are so many simple things to be aware of: a chicken to laugh at, a dog to pat, a kitten to fondle; there are always birds and boats to watch; the stages, houses, and docks are interesting; the hills, the pond and the road are exercising; there is the Light to look up to; and most wondrous of all, the ever-changing sea.

As each day passes more of the villagers are becoming individuals for me. When I came here they were all strangely alike, but now as they speak to me and I learn their names I seem suddenly to remember the first time I saw them. Many of the children are still just part of a lively assortment busy with play, they shyly hang their heads or run away when I speak to them; others seem to follow me around. The women timidly nod and smile as they pass me on the road. The mass of men around the stages is still something to hurry by without a glance, even the three who took me fishing have somehow merged with the rest – or kept out of my way. But when they are not lumped together, when I see them on the docks or in Alec's store, they speak to me, they answer my questions, they tease me about going fishing, about staying here longer than I intended – and the old ones ask me when I'm going to choose myself a man.

Every day after dinner I like to sit on the couch to stroke the faded cat and listen to the wrinkled old lady. "Poor pussy cat," she always says, "I love my pussy, I don't know how anyone could be unkind to animals," and she looks accusingly at Katie who says "Scat" when the cat tries to sneak into the pantry.

Today Mrs. Malcolm was aware of me and said, "You are far from home but the time it takes to get back is not long, not like it was when you had to wait for a sailing vessel. Sometimes we'd wait for weeks and weeks till the sea was calm enough to sail." The dim eyes turned toward the window where we could see the water. "It was a sad day when my father and brother were drowned. They went out in the morning and the sea washed over their boat. Other fishermen saw the wave that covered them and came home and told us. Strong men they were but they shed tears.

"My mother was left alone with nine children; she had all the man's work to do and all the woman's too. It was my eldest brother that was lost; the second boy, William, was apprenticed to learn a trade and my sister Elizabeth had such pretty amber hair, long and bright and curly." She smiled in recollection. "In Newfoundland you drew out a paper and paid so much money to give an apprenticeship. Mother had done that with William when he was nine years old. But the people who had him used him bad, he didn't get enough to eat and his clothes were no better than rags. Mother had to go to law to get him clear." The old woman rocked a while in silence.

"When I was a child we lived close to the sea, we used to run down on the sand in our bare feet and into the salt water. They never had to haul the boats ashore the way they haul them here, they anchored them near the land or tied them to the stages. In this place there is no shelter for ships or boats or people, I don't know why they call it a Harbour." Her hands gripped the arms of her chair. "I wish I'd died when I was young, then I'd have missed these long sad days; but no one died in Newfoundland, no one was ever sick; the women lived till they were old and the men were drowned at sea."

At four when the mail is sorted there's always a crowd in Alec's. This afternoon there was great excitement as well: Eaton's mail order catalogue had arrived and every family got a copy of the Wish Book or Winter Bible. The men took theirs home unopened, the women tore off the paper wrapping to get a quick look.

"Skirts is still short."

"Hope they got oilcloth in this, hadn't in the last one."

"I wants to git Bobbie some snow boots."

"We needs a new kettle."

Matt Clipper, his catalogue under his arm, left the store when I did. "I believe it's the catalogues that's causing all the trouble in the world," he said as we walked down the road together. "You think it over and see if I ain't roight." He looked worried. "People don't read their Boible no more at all, they just sets and pages through the catalogue. They sees all the foine things hinto it and wants to have 'em and if they can't get 'em they's full o' misery instead o' bein' happy off with what they has got."

Matt jerked his head towards the houses of the village, "Women round 'ere ain't so much for style but young girls wants to wear thin stockings all through cold weather. They can't put nothing under 'em loike they should do and then they gits sick. Bert Budge's girl had information of the glands last winter and doctor said it was nothin' but bein' dressed so thin and she's got to wear fleece-lined. Bert had awful toime with that girl, cryin' and carryin' on 'cause she couldn't be dressed foolish loike all the rest." Matt sighed. "Terrible thing, ain't it? Never used to be loike that, it's just since the war. Fishermen's been makin' money for the first toime in their loife, real big money too, most of 'em's up to a thousand dollars a year and one or two must have near twice that. Those that's got the most is proud and those that ain't got so much wants it. We's gettin' greedy now we's gettin' rich." Matt stopped at his gate, lifted his cap and scratched his head thoughtfully. "Oi often thinks we was happiest during the depression. Nobody had nothin' then; I kep' my family of six livin' on two hundred dollars one year; nobody else had more than that neither, we all helped each other and we was good off. Now seems loike everybody's just for their own self, tryin' to git something more out of the catalogue than other feller's got."

Matt opened his gate and started up his path where his little girls were playing. Seeing the catalogue under his arm, they ran to him and asked for it. He turned back to me, "You see," he said, "even children looks at catalogue and wants dolls when it ain't Christmas."

Two girls in shorts were on the dock when I went down to watch the boats come in tonight. In my delight at seeing strangers my own age to whom I might talk about the Harbour, I must have overwhelmed them with my greeting: they listened to me as though I were daffy old Ben Gunn on Treasure Island. My ardour dampened, I stood by the fishermen like a veteran while they gutted a swordfish and the visitors grimaced and squealed as they jumped away from the splattering blood.

"I got a lopster, Hector," wispy-haired little Ada, leaning over the side of the dock with a pole, called to a middle-sized boy in a dory.

"Let's see how beeg 'e is." She held up a leggy wriggler by its back. Hector yelled, "'e's too small, chuck 'im back." The little girl tossed the lobster over the side and squatted to look for another. An older boy sneaked up behind her and wrenched the pole from her hands. "Young savage," she called him with an angry scowl then turned her attention again to the boy in the dory. "One right in under ye, Hector," she shouted.

"Son of a beetch," cried Hector as he lunged at the lobster and the see-sawing dory almost tipped him into the sea.

"Here comes the *Maggie P.*," someone called as a small boat entered the bay. "Got a swordfish." Ella Jane's boys were joyously thumped on the back when they landed.

Hector came over to the dock and held his dory against the cribbing while the boy with Ada's pole lowered himself into the stern. "Give them lopsters to Ada," Hector said to him – but Ada had slipped into the bow. "Git out," the boys yelled when they saw her. She pushed the boat sharply from the wharf and calmly sat.

Stout, dark little lighthouse-keeper Clipper picked out a solid bit of fish entrail to take to his dog, he put it on a table and someone threw it overboard. Quickly Mr. Clipper got into a dory and retrieved it then walked around and watched the activity on the dock with the dripping morsel hanging from a string.

When a boat from Glace Bay landed several fish I said to Matt Clipper that I was sorry one of *our* men hadn't caught them. He grinned, "I feels the same, but when somebody from Neil's Harbour gits one I'm just that proud I don't care who it is."

Molly's Freddie gave me an eyeball. The prettier tourist girl admired it and said to the child, "Get me one of those." He brought her a crystal sphere, she handed him a coin and walked off the dock with her friend. Freddie looked at the money in his palm. "She give me a quarter for a eyeball," he said.

"Them ain't worth money."

"No, Freddie, can't keep that, ye got to give it back," Tommy Seaforth said.

"Come with." Freddie and Tommy and two other little boys ran after the strangers.

"Here comes snapper boat: Kootch, Diddle, and Gerald got one."

"How can you tell?" I asked.

"Sword's stickin' above gunwale."

"How many lopsters did ye git?" someone asked the trio of children in the dory as they came alongside.

"Eleven, but we chucked 'em overboard except seven that was daid," Hector said.

"What are you going to do with them?" I asked Ada as she stuffed them into a sack.

"Cook 'em." She scrambled onto the dock. "You want some?"

Susan, who was standing by, turned to me, "We's goin' cook 'em to our house. You want taste? Come along when you's ready, house side o' Molly's."

When I arrived the two little girls had a fire blazing in the kitchen stove, the lobsters were boiling, and a host of children waited for a treat. "How do you know when they're finished?" I asked. Ada looked at Susan and giggled. "When laig falls off," she said. Susan poured the water out of the pot, dipped the red lobsters into a dishpan of cold water then plopped them on the oilcloth-covered table. We gathered round and I asked, "Do you eat everything?"

"All but part of the haid and the old woman," Ada told me.

"That's gut," Susan explained, "looks loike a old woman with apron onto 'er, green part's liver, red part's the gingerbread, all good to eat." She tore a lobster apart to show me – and that was the signal for Ada and Hector and Bobbie and Freddie and Chester and Arlie and Gwendoline to rip open the rest and generously share their illegal bounty with me. "Ain't them some good?"

CHAPTER ELEVEN

BE WAHTER COLD DOWN DERE, FREDDIE?

SUNDAY, AUGUST 19

You can tell when Sunday comes in Neil's Harbour: the boats are anchored though the sea is calm, the Point and the wharves are deserted, there are many people on the road. Little boys in clean jerseys look freshly scrubbed, little girls wear hats over proudly shining faces, men have changed their swordfishing caps for wool ones, their heavy clothes for cotton shirts and blue serge trousers, women wearing figured rayon dresses and straw hats carry hymn books. Everyone walks towards the little seaside church where the black-clad Anglican clergyman receives his flock with outstretched arms.

Across the road the white steepled church hiding amongst the spruces has no resident preacher. There are only a few Presbyterian families in the two villages; not Newfoundlanders and not fisherfolk, they are old Cape Bretonners and very proudly

Scotch: the Malcolms, Maclennans, the awesome rich McKays who own half the Cove, the doctor, and Gladdie Buchanan who works for the government and reads the *Atlantic Monthly*. The women are clannish and visit one another; though they live in the village, they seem to be not of it.

Our dinner was late today because we had to wait for the deaconess to be brought from Cape North after her service in the church there. She preaches to the Presbyterians of the Harbour and the Cove every other Sunday evening during the summer. Though often smiling with an exaggerated show of pleasure, her face is sadly disfigured by deeply puckered creases. She sighed as she took her place at the table, "There was only a handful at Cape North church today," adding with asperity, "so I gave them a good bawling out to make them feel ashamed of themselves."

Katie, serving our food from the kitchen stove, announced, "We're having chicken."

"Which one?" I asked.

Miss Laurie murmured, "The white rooster."

"Oh no, not the one that gave you so much pleasure?"

"We haven't had chicken for a long time," Katie said defensively. "We couldn't keep feeding him forever."

"But how will you know when to expect a guest?"

"The little brown rooster will crow on the steps now," Miss Laurie assured me.

I never thought I could enjoy eating anything I had known personally but I found the white rooster a very pleasant change from codfish.

There is an aimlessness about this afternoon. The men sit together by the stages or walk around as if looking for something to happen, women chatter on front stoops, young men and girls walk along the Road, children play carefully in their Sunday clothes.

Down on the fish wharf, looking at things in the water, five little boys are leaning over the edge. "Look at de baits," one screams as a school of minnows flashes past. "Jeez, can't them swim some pretty?"

"Dey's not swimmin', dey's just goin' along."

"See dat lopster down dere under 'at mess o' fish guts?"

"Wisht I had a pole; Chester, fetch a pole." The smallest boy runs to the shore.

"Dere's mack'rel."

"How can you tell?" I ask. They all stare at me as if I'd asked how they know a cow is a cow.

"No mack'rel where you live?" I'm asked.

"There's no water."

"No wahter atall?" My questioner is Arlie, Molly's son, seven years old. He is the boy who caught the bird on the windy day and he is not unlike a tern: his nose, a bit too long for his thin little pointed face, is a beak; his eyes are dark and bright; his hair, cut on the bias over his forehead, is like the black cap of the sea-bird; he has the same wild look of flight and freedom. "Can you walk anywheres and not go owerboard?" he asks me.

"Yes, there's just pavement and buildings."

"Moi jumpins, must be a funny place." He looks at me curiously, his head on one side.

"I sees a heel!" someone exclaims. We are kneeling, the slim little bodies are taut, the tanned faces eager. "See en down dere in de kalop?" It takes a moment for me to find the snaky body below the swaying kelp.

"Let's git en, Rhindrus."

"Dose heels be hard to keel."

"Here's rock." Freddie throws it. Freddie is Arlie's slightly older brother.

" 'e 'it en, rock were roight on en. Be 'e keeled?" Arlie shrieks with excitement.

"You got to have crow-bar to kill dem t'ings."

"My son, you'll never see dat heel again, when you hits 'em dey goes roight off as far as South Point." For a moment the children are still; I hear the gentle flip-flop of water against the cribbing of the dock.

"Cheesus, dere's dat cat," Arlie points excitedly to a white form floating near the shore. "She's swelled up beeg as a peeg, ain't she?"

"Be 'er guts hangin' out?" Freddie asks.

"Can't see en," Arlie answers.

"Now what'll 'appen to 'er?" Rhindrus wonders.

"Oh she'll go on up shore, floies will git onto 'er and she'll stink awful."

99

"How'd she get into the water?" I ask.

Arlie tells me. "Her were roight tame and they ketched 'er and put 'er in bag, put string round 'er and tied rock on. De bobbles come up and 'er drownded."

"Why did they do it?"

"Her eyes was stuck shut and her couldn't see none."

"Her were bloind," Freddie explains.

"Were awful thin too," says Rhindrus.

"But 'er's roight beeg and swole now, ain't she?" Arlie exults.

"Let's go to the other side," I suggest and the children follow me. "There's a big sword," I point to it in the water.

"Freddie, woman wants sword, go git en," Arlie says.

"Oh moi, ain't 'e a long one? I'll git a pole." Freddie runs off the dock.

"Once I ketched a skulkin and a flatfish," Arlie tells me.

"What's the difference?"

Arlie is dumfounded by my ignorance. "Don't you know?" He frowns. "Skulkin's got big fins and little horns loike on top," he wriggles two fingers on either side of his head. "Flatfish ain't."

"Dere's dat lopster down dere still eatin'," someone says.

"Lopsters got 'is teeth in 'is claws," Arlie tells me.

"No 'e ain't," Rhindrus scoffs.

"Well 'e got little lumps loike," Arlie argues. He looks at me, "You got lopsters where you's at?" The little boy shakes his head, nonplussed. Freddie has come back with a pole, a spike in one end, a long cord fastened to the other end. "Freddie where 'er belongs ain't got no wahter, no wharfs nor nutting, only housses," Arlie tells.

"No fishin'?" Freddie asks. "Where do you git fish to eat?"

"In a store."

"Fish in store? Must be some funny place."

Freddie, looking over the side of the dock, sees the lobster. "Look at dat little booger down dere, I'm goin' to git en." He is gleeful. "Arlie you hold rope and when I throws pole you 'ang on and pull back." Arlie holds the rope in his little fists, Freddie throws the long pole. The pole comes back.

"Freddie's owerboard," Arlie screams.

Freddie can't swim. Twelve feet of water. Should I go in after him? He comes to the surface. I thrust the pole into his hands. He grasps it. I reach down and pull him up. He sits on the dock shivering convulsively, water streaming from him. Arlie regards him quizzically then he drawls, "Be wahter cold down dere, Freddie?"

Feddie's teeth are chattering, his hair and face are dripping, he tries feebly to wring water from his Sunday clothes. "You'll ketch it," Arlie warns him; he looks frightened. Arlie turns to me, "Our sister Gwendoline were owerboard in winter; Grandad were on dock and 'e seed 'er red coat in wahter and 'e sayed, 'I believe dat's Gwendoline down dere.' 'e went up and called our Dad and when 'e fished 'er out Gwendoline were roight purple." Arlie looks at Freddie, "But 'er ketched it good when 'er droid out."

There was company in the kitchen when I came home for supper. A radiant young woman sat in the rocker by the front window, a large unbleached cotton tablecloth embroidered in vivid colours spread over her knees. Miss Laurie was holding out a corner of it. It's beautiful work, Ivey," she said, "when did you find time to do it with a new baby?"

"When Jack's away with boats in Dingwall there ain't so much to do, the baby sleeps a lot." She smiled at me shyly, "Do you want to take a chance?"

"She's selling chances on it, three for ten cents," Katie explained as she moved between the pantry and the stove. "I wouldn't want a fancy thing like that myself, it's too hard to iron."

"Some folks likes to use a pretty cloth for a wedding or a christening." The work-reddened hands opened a box of little cardboard squares with numbers on them. We exchanged tokens as the deaconess came into the room.

"What is this?" she asked with her too-eager smile.

"It's a raffle," I told her. She flinched at the word, the smile left her face, its creases deepened. "My dear young woman," she said solemnly to the fisherman's wife, "do you realize what you are doing?" The sweet face looked up at her, bewildered. The deaconess asked, "Don't you know that gambling is a sin?"

"But I don't gamble." There was surprise in the young mother's voice. "My man maybe plays a little poker in the stages but there ain't no harm to it."

The eyes of the deaconess were not compassionate. "My be-

101

loved Christian friend," she said sharply, "that embroidery is the work of the devil."

Folding up her cloth the village woman rose from her chair with composed indignation, "Oh no, it ain't," she said, "I worked it myself, every stitch, to make money for a new linoleum in my kitchen."

After supper Arlie was waiting for me outside my gate. I walked towards the Point and he followed at a distance of five paces. We paused to talk about a cow, walked round a dazzling blue sedan that blocked the narrow road. "Some shoiny, ain't 'e?" Arlie observed.

"What koind o' people be them?" the child wondered as a tense little grey man and a bloated young one got out and wandered aimlessly towards the Light. Unlike Harbour men, who keep their shirts tucked in, they wore their loud figured ones hanging over their slacks. A grey-haired, well-groomed woman and a pretty petulant young one emerged from the back of the car and stared at Arlie and me. "What a quaint little boy," the older one gushed and looked towards me for comment. Arlie picked up a stick and ran after a dog. No longer feeling inclined to act as Hostess of the Harbour, I went without a word to sit on the porch steps with Alec and a fisherman who were watching the Presbyterians of the village go to evening service.

"Elsa's gone, aren't you going?" Alec asked me.

"I can't, I haven't a hat."

Alec teased, "Seems odd a woman can't go to church because she hasn't a hat."

"It is so, ain't it?" the fisherman spoke. "Women only wears hats in church and that's only place men takes theirs off."

Charlotte Clipper, on her way from fetching milk at the Malcolms, invited me to come home with her. Like all the houses I've seen in the Harbour her's was shining and tidy, with linoleum and hooked mats on the floor and pictures of sailing vessels on the walls. The front room had a large new chesterfield suite which invited admiration.

We were in the dining room having lime juice, layer cake, and blueberry pie when Charlotte's husband, Big Jim, came in from the shore. "Whoi ain't you in front room?" he asked as he sat with us at the table.

"We was," Charlotte told him.

"Did she like the set?" he asked eagerly.

"Yes, she sat on the chesterfield and she says it's grand."

"It just come on *Aspy* two weeks ago," he explained to me. "It'll be roight comfable to set on when winter comes."

"In winter you sets by kitchen stove," his wife said firmly.

Jim lit his pipe. "Charlotte show 'er the bottle that pours out four kinds o' liquor." She fetched an empty divided decanter. "I got that in St. Pierre," Jim said. "You heard o' St. Pierre and Miquelon, ain't you? Islands south of Newfoundland, belongs to France. A grand place with buildings and lots to drink. French people are great for sellin' things: most of their trade is liquor, they'll let you taste what you moight fancy to buy and afore you know it you're daid drunk." Jim smiled in recollection. "You should see some o' them Frenchmen, they wears flat round caps loike and some has wooden shoes. Awful religious they is, great for parades and that. I seen little girls marching with whoite dresses and veils onto 'em, pretty as blossoms. And they got the foolishest graveyard you could ever see, has cement boxes with portholes into 'em and if you look in you can see the coffins where the daid is laid in."

Charlotte shuddered, "Ain't that awful?"

"There used to be a lot o' runnin' back and forth during prohibition, bringin' in rum. Police watched pretty close all the toime but still they brought it in handy enough. Wouldn't moind havin' another trip up there one day," Jim rubbed his chin reflectively and Charlotte breathed a sigh. I said, "I wish I could go too."

"You wants to do a lot o' things, don't you?" Charlotte said.

"We'll git Calvin to take ye codfishin'," Jim laughed. "Ye know mother, we's tryin' to make a match between Calvin and this girl," he tittered and Charlotte shook her head.

"Poor Calvin," I said, "you love to tease him, don't you?"

" 'e knows it's all in fun," Jim sputtered. "You'd never know Calvin were sixty-eight year old, would you?"

"I thought he might be fifty."

"That's it and if ye ever seen 'im cleaned up you'd git a real surprise," Jim said. "He never shaves, you know, except for a funeral. He lives by himself in his sawmill and gits pretty dirty but he's a roight foine man and can look good too if 'e wants to.

His sister died down in Sydney and Calvin come up here fer me to shave 'im -never done it hisself in his loife - 'e had a tie with him that I gave 'im the last toime 'e went to a burying and 'e wanted me to put it on 'im because 'e didn't know how to tie it. I threw it in foire and got 'im another one. Well 'e had on his serge suit and after I got 'im shaved 'e went up the hill to have a look at old Mr. Bickford that just doid. We forgot all about 'im and when we seen a man in a blue suit coming down the hill I says, 'Who's that now?' And Mother says, 'Must be a stranger.' Well, sir, it were Calvin! We just didn't know 'im atall, 'e looked that smart."

CHAPTER TWELVE

WAITIN' FER A CAM

MONDAY, AUGUST 20

The deaconess is taking a long time in the bathroom; I am waiting at the window of my room watching the horse population of
the Harbour in its favourite morning spot between Alec's store
and a stage. Four mares have lined up with their heads across
one another's shoulders, perfectly spaced as if they'd been trained
for an equine act. Miss Laurie's cow is at the gate, trying to lift
the latch with her brown velvet nose; I wonder if she's conscious
of the flicking of her tail, I wonder what she thinks as she chews
her cud.

It's fun to muse about the cows that wander in the Harbour. I
always thought cows the most banal of creatures but here they
look at me with insolent composure: a brindle brown with hum-
py hips has an air of bored sophistication, she gazes with the arrogance of a dowager through lorgnette; a spotted white one is a

snob; across from Alec's house a sleek big black one lies enthroned upon a hillock, her blasé stare makes me feel uncomfortably gauche – and Arlie says she gives black milk.

The boats have not gone out today, they bounce on waves in the bay. I can't escape the wind, it finds me wherever I hide. The fishermen are restive too, they look at the sky and the water, they sit on the grass, go into the stages, and walk along the roads.

Since I was a child I've thought fishermen were weather prophets. I've believed rhymes about "Red Sky at Morning," and "When the Wind is from the North"; now I am disillusioned. All the little battery radio sets in the Harbour are kept tuned to the Maritime station that gives a detailed prediction of weather. Morning and evening I see the men squinting as they look at the sea and the sky. "Goin' to blow?" they ask one another. "Forecast says nardly." And that settles it. Matt Clipper told me the weather this summer has been unusually capricious; if there had been a good storm this spring the water would all come one way instead of blowing in every direction with every changing wind. "Jest loike a woman," he said with a grin. I look at Matt's blue eyes and wonder if fishermen's eyes are blue from looking so long at the sea.

As a tall old man with glasses and a long ragged moustache came towards us on the road, Matt said, "Now here's somebody for you to meet, me father, John Clipper, eighty-two year old and buildin' boats all hisself. Show 'er your boats, Dad," he called. "This girl wants to know everything."

"I often seen you around," the old man said as we walked along. "Always writin', ain't you?" he smiled. "Must be noice to write." He opened the door of a stage near the water's edge and we went in. "I never went to school; just when I should a gone, teacher went down to Sydney and started a shoe factory. So I never got learnin'. I might ha' if my woife hadn't a died, she could read straight off and I picked up enough letters from her so I could read one chapter out o' the Bible clear through." The old man shook his head, "Never could understand 'im though."

Inside the stage was a green fishing boat. "Twenty-three foot long, seven-foot beam and thirty-two-inch draft." Mr. Clipper repeated her proportions. "I guess I built twenty or more o' them boats, caulked and painted, real fishin' boats they is. I made ten-ton snapper boats too, takes a lot o' figgerin' when you don't know numbers. I'm workin' on another one outside," he nodded towards a boat down the road, "when it's fair I works on she, when it's dirty I works in stage."

"Are you going to use them yourself?"

"They's for me sons. I give up fishin' last year when me laig got sciatic; doctor says there's no harm to it, I'm good for bein' a hunnert like me mother. Her's spry as a mack'rel and still smart; in winter makes crib quilts fer Hospital Auxilary, goes reglar for Alec to cash her Old Age cheque; last time, to tease 'er, 'e kep' some back and she sayed, 'Alec, you're not givin' me enough, it wants another dollar.'"

Dinner was delayed again today. The deaconess said, "Sorry I'm late, I've been distributing tracts all morning." She sighed wearily as she sat with Miss Laurie and me at the dining room table – Katie was eating in the kitchen so she wouldn't miss her radio serial. "Sometimes I think I'll never be able to change people," the deaconess said. The creases in her face deepened. "When was the Finney girl married?"

"In June." Miss Laurie's smile was wistful. "She has a lovely baby, she takes such good care of it."

"It shouldn't have come before she was married."

"It came when it was ready, I'm sure," Miss Laurie's mouth was prim.

"I thought Elva Finney was a nice girl, she should be ashamed to show her face after carrying on the way they do around here."

"Neil's Harbour young folk always take their trouble. Elva had a wonderful wedding," Miss Laurie told us, "everyone in the Harbour and the Cove got a hand-written invitation. We couldn't got but we saw the bridal party walk past on the way to the church; the bride in a long white dress and veil, the brides-maids in pink and blue. And they say the feast at the Finneys' was the best ever given in the Harbour, the young people danc-ed until morning and the baby slept through it all."

Sam Hatch came to the house after dinner to buy a couple of eggs. He is the homely man who asked me to enlarge his snapshot. A bachelor, living by himself, he seems to have no place in the village; he is not a fisherman, he has no skill – though they say he makes moonshine for his own enjoyment – he is an unnecessary person; I see him always alone.

Keeping his shapeless tweed cap on his head, he asked me about my drawing, then sat on the little chair just inside the kitchen door and politely asked Mrs. Malcolm about her health. With the arrogance of age, she ignored him.

"I see you ain't usin' the cane I made for you," he shouted to overcome her deafness. The old lady rocking in her chair didn't seem to hear him. "I knew she was needin' a stick so I tied a knot in a little sapling I seen in the woods and made a fine cane of it for her," he told me.

Katie handed me a varnished stick with a smooth round knob on one end. "It's too long for her, she's never been able to use it."

"I can fix that," Sam said, taking it from me. "I done that some years ago." He fondled its smoothness. "I done a lot of things, I spend all my time workin' and sleepin' and readin' stories, but I git tired of that; there's nothin' in it when you've done it so long. I worked on the railway, on the telegraph lines, and now I'm painting Alec's house."

"Are you getting anywhere with it?" the old lady asked.

Sam Hatch looked surprised, "No, I ain't, I ain't gettin' nowhere. I often think I'd been better off if I done something wrong and got sent to Dorchester prison where I could have learned a trade; I read about men going in places like that and doing right good when they come out. This way I don't learn nothing."

"Why didn't you stay in Sydney when you were working there?" Katie asked.

Sam looked stricken. "They can have the city life," he almost shouted. "Nobody can sit still or be alone there. They're all jumpin' around. Where I boarded there was two young girls always runnin' out to a show or a dance or drinking beer; they'd stay late then come home and turn on the radio real loud, seemed they was always wantin' a noise so nobody could think. I believe they was afraid to be quiet. I like to be still and alone – so I come back to Neil's Harbour. I like to walk by myself in the night and look at the stars."

"And what do you think about then?" I asked him.

"About Eternity mostly, wondering if there's anything in the Hereafter . . ." he turned to me, "ever think about that?" But before I could answer he jumped up and ran out the door.

"His father was daft too," the old lady explained.

"Whenever the moon was full he used to put on a stiff hat and walk for miles along the shore," Katie added.

"I used to walk for miles and miles along the shore when I was home in Newfoundland." The old lady started rocking again, her lamentation was timed to the slow rhythm of the movement of her chair. "No one knows how terrible, no one knows how sad it was when a man went out to sea in the morning and never came back again." She keened as she rocked. "No one knows, no one knows." The dim eyes sought my face as I sat on the couch. "Since you came to us the sun has been shining, the wind has been soft and the sea has been calm, but the wind can be wild and the sea can be cruel, deathly cruel," she rocked to her words. "It has taken the bravest, taken the best. I remember when the *Harmony* went down. In 1868 it was and only one was saved." She stopped rocking. "He jumped into the longboat and crashed on the rocks off-shore. For two days and nights he clung there with not even a mitt to warm him. When the storm was spent they fetched him in, still breathing. Mrs. Sweet nursed him all winter, nursed him till April came. She wrote a poem about it:

"The ninth night of November, most dreadful for to know,
We struck a rock in Newfoundland, which caused our overthrow.
The watch called out, 'All hands on deck your precious lives to save,'
But out of nine you soon shall find, . . . you soon shall find," the old mind faltered.

"Eight sunk beneath the waves," Miss Laurie prompted.

"Our noble captain gave commands the lashing to cut away,
'The boat she is going down,' unto his men did say
And one man in the longboat, from the wreck got washed away,
The last he saw the Captain, was on the mast so high," the old woman rocked faster.

"The brig went down with a dismal sound and never more saw I. That's all I know of that."

This afternoon I climbed the little road winding up the hill amongst the houses and walked beyond them to the barrens. Running over and round great rocks, I found a labyrinth of paths half hidden by low bushes – and Neil's Harbour spread out like a map below me.

From the height I could see that every fisherman's house in the village is like a watchtower perched on the slope of the high treeless hill. From all the front windows can be seen everything that goes on along the roads, on the wharves and on the sea to the far horizon. The back and side windows give intimate glimpses of small barns, outhouses and the little paths that have been beaten through the rocky fields from one house to another. There is little privacy in the Harbour; everyone knows everything that goes on there; though there are no phones, news is carried more quickly over the network of paths, even when they are muddy or thigh-deep in snow drifts.

Neil's Harbour is just like a family: every one of its three hundred people is a cousin or uncle or aunt of somebody else in the village – except the Presbyterians, the merchant, the doctor and the Anglican preacher. There are at least sixty Clippers; two-thirds of the rest are Seaforths, Candles, Patsons, Williams, Buffets and Budges.

On my way down from the barrens I stopped to talk with a soldier sitting on a fence rail. He had just come back from overseas occupation duty, he told me, and during several years in the army – including World War II – he had seen places from Korea to Berlin, and always he wanted to come back to his own little village to fish as his father and grandfather had done.

But with the large trawlers and draggers from all the world catching cod near Cape Breton's shores, the little boats of Neil's Harbour have scant market for their comparatively small supply of fish; the children of the fishermen must leave their homes and go inland or join the army. "Fifteen boys from this little place have joined up because they can't make a living here and got no education to make it somewhere else. And this ain't the only place neither: all round Nova Scotia you can see houses rotting down, abandoned by their folks that couldn't make it go."

The young man stared gloomily at the water. "I'm tired of

soldiering but I don't want to work in a city, all pavement and buildings with cars and people running around, all rushing and crowding; people got such big ideas about themselves in the city because everything there is man-made, even the grass and the trees is man-planted. Man gets to thinking he's God-almighty," the soldier looked all around him, "here where there's nothing much but sea and sky, he knows damn well he ain't."

Despite the high wind the heat is oppressive today. I'd feel much better if I could use Katie's pink soap in the pond but she says the sand blowing along the beach would cut my eyes and the tide near the rocks would carry me away. What the soldier said about a city may be true but there are times when I yearn for its greatest convenience – a bathtub with running water.

On my way home for supper I met Henry Rider carrying a bucket. "You still here?" he asked me.

"Yes, I can't seem to leave."

"That's the same as it were with me, now my old woman come ower from Newfoundland and I'll never get away."

I don't know what it is about shambling old Henry that brings a lump to my throat. And not only Henry but all the people who live in the Harbour. They are so natural, so unaffected and honest, like children before they learn too much from grownups of proper finicky ways. I love the way they talk, the things they say, I love their quiet faces, their slow sureness in everything they do. And their kindness.

I am learning a new way of life in Neil's Harbour: a way that is uncomplicated by unnecessary values, serene yet exciting, humble, unworried and fun; there is drama but it is not dramatized, love that is not romanticized, beauty that is not eulogized; there is security in man's own resourcefulness and ability to be grateful for necessities.

Miss Laurie told me of a woman on the hill whose husband died last fall: every man in the village who went to cut wood in the forest brought a portion for the widow so she'd have enough to last all winter, and they chopped it for her too. When anyone is ill people prepare food and do the work that the sick one can't do; everyone seems anxious to help someone else and I've heard no one talk about nerves!

111

Yet I'm still finding it hard to relax, even here in the village where it should be the easiest thing in the world with the example set by all the old men who sit against the stages whittling a bit of shingle, and the little boys who curl up and sleep in a derelict rowboat or on the sun-warmed boards of a dock. I can't settle down and quietly read *War and Peace*: I have to keep running around; I don't want to waste my precious time here.

I am also learning the feeling of a man who gallivants. I do almost the same thing every evening at the Harbour. The Malcolms go to bed at dusk; the flickering oil lamp in my room is too dim to read by, so I walk along the Road – not because I want to but there is nothing else I can do.

Tonight when I passed young men sitting on the bank I heard one of them say, "I always liked a red-head." I paid no attention but two of them ran ahead and blocked my way. "Would you like some gum?" one offered, a tall fair lad with crooked teeth whom I had often seen on the dock; the other was a thin little fellow with a bold look.

"I thought you was going home?" the thin one said.

"Don't go, there's a Time tomorrow night," the tall one grasped my arm. I pulled away and walked out of their sight.

Where the water comes close to the road I sat on the grass, listening to the rattle of the stones as the combers rolled them in and out on the floor of the sea. Two girls smoking cigarettes said hello as they passed by me; one was Maggie Patson, the other was Nellie Candle. A man coming from the Cove said goodevening. A horse, sauntering along, came close to me. The girls walked back to say, "It looks like rain." Almost at once the boys who had stopped me were sitting on either side. "Nice night, ain't it?" one said. The girls ran giggling away.

"I'll take ye codfishing tomorrow evening," the big boy said.

"What time?" I asked him.

"One o'clock, you be on wharf. Have ye got a pair of nippers?"

"What are nippers?"

"Gloves without fingers so you won't git blisters from handline. Your hands look awful soft," the thin boy tried to hold one.

"You stay outa this, Fin," said the big one, "her's goin' wi' me."

"I didn't say I'd go."

"You scared?"

Both boys stood up and left me alone at the side of the road. An embracing couple passed. The girls came back to ask if I'd like to walk with them. Maggie took my hand; Nellie took Maggie's; they swung their arms as we kept in step on the road. They told me they work all day, the Road is their greatest pleasure. "But soon I'll be walkin' on sidewalks and lookin' at store windows in Toronto," Maggie exulted, and we talked of what she might expect in the city.

Near the school we met three boys who clasped the girls and kissed them. "Git away ye little brat," Nellie slapped one.

When darkness came we had reached the Cove and turned back towards the Harbour. "Wait for me," a man's voice called after we'd passed the corner. The big blond fisherman was walking close behind us. "What you want, Gaff?" Maggie asked him.

"I'll take the red-head." We stopped walking.

"He wants you to go grassing," my new friends informed me.

"What is grassing?"

"You better go and find out," the girls giggled and disappeared up the bank in the darkness.

The boy took my arm, "Come wi' me, dear."

Curious, yet resisting, I let him pull me up a little path. "Where does this lead?" I quavered.

"To the Presbyterian Church." It was a wooded way with a scent of spruces and wintergreen; it wound past a yard where tombstones showed, round the back of the House of God. "Grass be nice and thick right here, the best there is in Neil's Harbour."

"It feels quite soft," I said as we sat. I moved when he sprawled beside me.

"You shy?" He lessened the space between us; it broadened again as I shifted.

"I'm shy too." He put his arm around me. "Don't go home so soon, my dear."

"Let me go," I struggled.

"Don't ye know I'm crazy for ye? I been after ye since ye come here."

"No, please . . ."

"No harm to try."

I found the path in the darkness. He called as he ran behind me. "Be ye 'fraid I'll knock ye up?"

CHAPTER THIRTEEN

GIRL WANTS TO WRITE BOOK ABOUT WE

TUESDAY, AUGUST 21

Oh glorious day! I'm full of zest and zeal and Zion! I'm so excited I can hardly hold my pencil! I woke half an hour ago knowing I'm going to do a marvellous thing – I'm going to try to write a book about Neil's Harbour. I'm bursting to talk about it and no one could listen to all I want to tell; I've always wanted to write and at last I have something wonderful to write about.

I'll have to be terribly organized:

1. Write my family that I must stay a week longer.
2. Wire Halifax for my mail.
3. Make lists of things to learn about the Harbour.
   (a) It must have an interesting history.
   (b) Find out about the shipwrecks.
   (c) There is sure to be buried treasure.
   (d) Ask about the different kinds of fishing and its hazards.

(e) I'll go out on that damn water till I see them catch a swordfish, and I'll catch some cod.

When I think of all these things I'm so thrilled I feel nervous.

Eager to start asking questions, I walked to the Point after breakfast. There wasn't a soul to be seen. I strolled down the road, stopping by a fence where Elsa's tiny Marie with eyes like blue flowers was looking through the pickets. "Wheah goin'?" she asked me. A big brown mongrel came to have his ears rubbed, he sniffed my hair and made a satisfied sound. "What's 'e sayin'?" Marie wanted to know. A big fisherman went by and called "Hello, dear," to Marie.

Arlie came next, bare-footed, his tousled head bent over a blackened tin can. "Want sniles?" he asked me, jabbing into the can with a hooked piece of wire. "Got 'em hangin' on fish dock, made foire on shore and cooked 'em into can wi' sea water." As he talked he pulled out of a little spiral shell a wormy grey slug that looked like what might have gone into or come out of a robin. He offered it to me. I looked at the rusty tin, at Arlie's grimy hands, his gamin face, and thought, "He'll probably live to be a healthy old man." I gulped the snail. Arlie's eyes crinkled when he grinned, "Ain't them some good?"

The smells around the shore were more pungent in today's heat: very old lobster bait, dried fish bones, cod livers in a vat really *stank!* The dock had a smell of its own from all the fish that have been gutted there; my crepe rubber soles stuck to the encrusted blood and pulled off with a *swoosh.*

"Some warm today," a very old codfisherman said as he landed, "hottest day we ever had in our loife."

"You should wear shorts," I teased him. He laughed and said, "We always wears fleece-lined, summer or winter, never changes 'em. We sweats but it soaks in and dries off; when snow comes we stop sweatin' but we don't feel the cold; weather's all the same to we, never feels it through our clothes."

Five young boys in bathing trunks, their legs and bodies white as foam, forearms and faces brown, emerged from a stage near the dock. One of them was Tommy Seaforth; seeing me, he crossed his arms over his bare chest and ducked behind a pile of lobster traps. The rest screamed as they splashed each other in the shallow water near the shore. "You supprised them can't swim?" Big Jim asked me. "Not many in Harbour be swimmers. Ain't no one to learn 'em. I ain't been in water for ower twenty year myself."

"Why don't you go?" I asked.

He gave an embarrassed laugh, "We used to go in our bare buff but when tourists started comin' in cars it weren't never the same."

The men on the dock are too busy splitting cod to tell me things in the organized way that I need for the book. I must talk to them when they sit idly around the stages. But how can I approach that formidable mass that stops its conversation whenever I come along? I know it is partly made up of men who have spoken to me alone but the thought of their solidarity makes my muscles stiffen whenever I go near them.

Which of course is silly.

When I question them about their life in the Harbour they tell me generously all that I want to know. There is hardly an hour I am with them that I do not feel we are one and the same as we talk and laugh and they tease me and we watch the sky and the sea.

Yet when they ask me questions about the place I come from, they listen to my answers with a look of diffidence or suspicion. Sometimes as I wander around the Harbour I feel it is heaven and home, at other times I think I would always be alien among its people.

I walked slowly down the avenue of stages with my notebook. In the gathering of men standing at the side of the road I saw Matt Clipper. I stopped in front of him and said, "Matt, will you help me with something?"

"Sure, what can Oi do fer ye?"

"I want to know all about the different kinds of fishing."

A tall rangey middle-aged man with teasing blue eyes stood beside Matt. "What you doin' all the time with that book?" he asked me. "You ain't goin' waste all that paper, you're goin' write something on it, ain't you?"

I was trapped. "I want to write a book about Neil's Harbour," I admitted.

"About Neil's Harbour? Whatever for? Ain't nothin' interesting here."

"I'd like to tell about it so everyone can know how wonderful it is."

The men looked solemn for a moment, then Matt Clipper said, "Oi believe that's a good thing, lots people come 'ere and talk loike they thinks we be savages."

"That's right, some comes and looks at we like we be dirty," an unshaved fisherman said.

"Some thinks they's way better'n we," an older one spoke. "They thinks they's more civilized 'cause they got more."

Matt Clipper said to me, "Now you tell us what you want."

"I'm afraid I'll have to ask a lot of questions."

"That's all roight, you got to ask to foind out. We'll tell ye, we'll all tell ye, won't we, men?" Matt was enthusiastic, the others looked a bit uncertain.

"Of course you know the book might never be published, I've never written a book and I don't know how to do it, but if I put down what you tell me something may come of it."

"If you really want the best, you ask Jack Torrence," Matt indicated the tall rangey man. "He just about knows everything. He's smart as any lawyer. Don't know how he got so smart, only went to second grade in school, started fishin' when 'e were ten year old, but no one can best 'im in anything."

"Does he read much?"

"The *Sydney Post*. And he can tell you the Bible clear through. He don't read nothin' else, yet 'e seems to know it all." As soon as his eulogy started, the tall fisherman walked up the road away from us. "Now who?" I asked Matt.

"Come on ower 'ere to Tom Candle's stage; he's mendin' 'is naits and man mendin' naits always got lots o' company. You'll soon foind out all you wants." We walked to the ramp of the weathered shack and Matt said, "Here's girl wants to write book about we so us got to tell 'er what to put hinto it."

From the darkness inside someone said, "George, git off that kag and let the lady have it." A man ran down the plank and I sat on the little keg in the doorway. The windows of the stage were boarded, there was light only near the entrance where I saw Tom Candle half covered with netting: a short stocky man, about sixty, with a round face and shining cheeks dimpled by a toothless grin; dropping his chin to the collar of his plaid flannelette shirt, he peered at me over his round steel-rimmed glasses with earnest blue eyes. "Now what does ye want to know?"

"All about the fishing."

"Don't ye know nothin'?"

"Not much."

He turned towards the darkness in the stage, "Well men, bein's how she ain't no more stuck up ner we be, I'll show 'er how a herrin' gits ketched." My eyes becoming accustomed to the gloom, I saw two men in swordfishing caps, one sitting on a backless chair, the other on a trestle table, and on another keg, friendly old Uncle Joe holding a grandchild on his knee. Beyond them in the space about twenty by twelve feet, I had a hazy impression of a row boat, barrels, kellicks, bobbers and lobster traps.

Tom Candle went to a barrel in a corner and from it brought a glinting silver fish dripping brine. He took his net in one hand, held the fish as far away from it as his arms would stretch, and said, "See 'ere 'e is, swimmin' along like this," wobbling the stiff wet fish in the air, " 'e comes up to nait, don't see it, puts 'is haid through hole," Tom demonstrated what he was saying, " 'e tries to go through but 'e can't, tries to back out but 'is gills is ketched so 'e gits drownded." Tom dropped the corners of his mouth and sagged his shoulders while the men laughed at his imitation. "Herring drowns easiest of any of 'em." He jerked the fish from the net and returned it to the barrel. "Naits is kep' out all the time, we hauls 'em up every morning and picks out fish like flies in a spider's web."

"Nets is twenty-one fathom long and four fathom deep," the man on the table told me. "Sometimes a big fish gits all rolled up in net and tears it to pieces."

"Remember the blackfish I had?" Tom Candle turned towards the man. "Like a small whale a blackfish is, they come up and blow; we stays clear of 'em," he told me. "One in me nait weighed ower a ton, slashin' and rilin' the water 'e was, I couldn't tackle 'im so I goes and gets men in 'nother boat but soon as we come up to 'im away 'e goes quicker'n hell." Tom spat tobacco juice over his net. "I'm still mendin' them holes."

"What is the first fish you go after in spring?"

"First is cod, soon as the hice is gone and we can git the bait –

herrin' ketched like I showed you. Codfish we catches with trawls." Tom turned to someone I hadn't noticed reclining in the rowboat. "Young feller, go up in loft and bring down trawl, I guess this girl ain't never seed one."

A trawl appeared to be a small wooden tub full of a mess of thin rope and fish hooks. Tom Candle picked up the trawl line – which strangely enough wasn't tangled at all – and showed me that every forty-two inches there hung a two-foot cord with a hook on the end of it. "Trawl be baited every evening for next mornin's fishin', we let it out o' boat while we's goin' along and leaves it about two hours fer a day setting or all night, then we hauls it in. One man puts trawl in tub and other takes fish off; we clear two thousand hooks in two hours every day it ain't blowin' from April till mid July when swordfishin' starts. We don't bother with naits or trawls during swordfishin' season – too many boats might run into 'em – but end of September we put 'em out again."

"Lots o' waitin' round in this swordfishin' business, waitin' fer a cam," Uncle Joe drawled. "Some boats ain't made a cent yet."

"Swordfishin' be a change, more like sport or playing poker – once you start it, you can't quit," the man on the table said.

"What about lobster fishing?"

"Lopsters is the best money; we couldn't live without lopster fishin' but too many's in it," Tom told me. "Everybody that's got a boat or even a dory goes after lopsters. You should see them wharfs week before season starts on May 15, piled high as ye can reach 'em wi' lopster traps. It's just like a race to see who can put their's into boat first and be on their way. We sinks traps just clear of shore in water to twenty fathoms. We visits 'em every morning, hauls 'em up to boat, takes lopsters out o' parlour, puts bait on spindles and lowers 'em down again. Them with most traps gits maybe three hundred pounds but lots o' days it's too rough to go after 'em. One year we lost all our traps in a storm."

"Lopsters is gettin' smaller every year," Uncle Joe said. "Oi moind when Oi were fishin' they was three-four pound."

"Not many comes that big. We sells 'em to canning factory in Cove, they pays the leastes' but we got no way to git 'em out from

119

here live." Tom held up his net to look for more holes. "Soon as lopster fishin's over July 15, we gits ready for swordfishin'."

"When do you get mackerel?"

"Mackerel comes up this way in spring but it's no good, thin and got a scum over its eyes; by summer it's fat and we use small hook and handline over side o' boat and hook 'em fast as we can haul 'em in. By first November they's gone and we fish cod till drift ice comes end o' January; you can't see no salt water atall then, just ice high as housses."

"It don't get so cold here but sometimes it's terrible wild," the man on the chair said. "Comes a nor'easter we stay in house three or four days."

"Some years ago we used to fish wi' two-stemmers; fine boats they was, bigger'n ours is now, but a storm smashed 'em to pieces, twenty-six in one night." Tom shook his head. "My dear woman, 'twas a horrible sight when we come down in the mornin' and all our boats was nothin' but kindlin' wood in the water."

"It was so," the man on the chair agreed. "A terrible, terrible thing."

"See that boat out there?" the man on the table pointed to a schooner anchored in the bay, "Feller into it had a hawful hexperience 'ere last year; 'e had boat worth two thousand dollars with half a ton o' fish on board and were on 'is way to Glace Bay where 'e comes from, when a snow storm come up and 'e couldn't see where 'e were goin'. Afore long 'is boat foundered onto 'im and they had to put out in dory. The sea carried 'em a-long and landed 'em on only strip o' beach fer a mile either way, the rest were sheer cliff."

"They didn't save theirselves that time, I guess," Tom Candle's eyes rolled piously upward, "it were the Man up above did it for 'em. Their big boat were battered to matchwood."

"The good Lord saved you too when shark near got you," Uncle Joe said.

Tom stopped working on his net to tell me: "Couple year ago when we was haulin' lopster traps we seen shark long as our boat with 'is haid out o' water and 'is teeth showing white and sharp-pointed, a wickeder sight you never could see, and comin' right for us. I threw gas can at en and gas spread on top o' water; shark didn't like the taste o' that, 'e dived but 'e kep' coming right after us. 'e broke propeller shaft in two; engine stopped, and there we was." Tom passed his hand across his forehead. "Quick I grabbed the long-handled gaff and throwed it straight through 'is guts. He went under boat and rised it clear out o' water. We prayed fast and hung on till she come down again, floating. There was blood on the water and shark were gone."

Table: "He'd a comed aboard sure if you hadn't throwed that gaff."

Chair: "He'd a spilled you out and et you."

Big Jim Clipper, passing by, called to me, "You gotta look out fer Tom there, 'e's woife's away an' 'e's an awful feller for the women."

Tom's grin showed his toothless gums. He said, "I never had a drop o' liquor in me life but I loves to chase the women." He wagged his finger at me. "What you should do is go after feller owns sawmill, Calvin Leaf: he's a bachelor, got lots o' money and cats. You likes cats and money is handy." He spat. "Money's awful thing though, ain't it? You can't eat it, can't drink it, but you can't live without it. The more people's got the more they wants; the rich is the worst for it, the poor ain't after it so wild."

Table: "They takes the Old Age Pension soon as they can git it."

Because Tom Candle's stage is placed on a slight crook in the avenue of stages its doorway commands a long view of the road from the Trail. As he worked and talked, Tom, peering over his specs, kept watching everything that moved. "There goes a Newfoundlander into Alec's; can always tell a Newfoundlander by the walk, they seems to be hove down more than any other: the lazy walkers, I calls 'em, though they's the hardest workers in the world." There was a lull in our conversation till Tom exclaimed, "Look, look at crowd in that car. Pity some Chinaman ain't here with a restaurant, 'e'd make a pile o' money."

Chair: "Too hard to git meat fer it; meat's been some scarce this summer. I'd fancy a bit o' meat one o' these days, ain't tasted nothin' but fish for near three weeks."

Tom: "Be better in winter, t'ousands o' pattridges in ma'shes this year, I'm thinkin'."

Chair: "If foxes don't get 'em. More foxes this year than rabbits; they come out brazen and look right at you."

Table: "Lots o' deer too; I likes deer meat in winter."

Me: "What else do you have then?"

Tom: "Well it wouldn't seem like Saturday if we didn't have baked beans for supper. Sundays we has boiled taties, cabbage, salt or fresh meat and puddin'; always beans for breakfast."

Table: "Sometimes we has heggs 'n jam-bread, 'n cornmeal porridge; some mornings it's dried fish and taties with pork fat fried out and onions boiled together; we soak the fish night before and us men gets it ready ourself."

"Keep still, Alfie, you can't pee in here, you gotta go outside," Uncle Joe said sharply to his grandson who was jiggling up and down.

Tom: "Fer supper we 'ave fish or fish cakes made o' leftovers or hash made from boiled dinners, or pancakes. We eats good. Trouble wif people nowdays is they eats too light food."

Table: "Tom, you goin' shave fer bean feed tonight?"

Tom: "No, I only shaves on Saturday. Too hot fer bean feed but I'll go and chase the women." He grinned wickedly at me. "You want to look out fer me, I'm a terrible, terrible man."

A voice sang out:

"Allemande left, allemande right,
All join hands in the centre, fall."

The dancers whirled in the moonlight.

"On to your partners, corners address,
Join your hands and away to the west."

A speechless, plain young man took my hand and led me to the platform: from one pair of arms to another, I was pulled through the measures of the Square. Among the bystanders a childish voice called out, "You're doin' roight good, Aidna."

At eleven the women were cleaning the bean pots, the dancing was less brisk, a drunken soldier challenged a drunken fisherman to a fight. I walked homeward with Maggie Patson and Nellie Candle.

At the bean feed my big blond swain of the churchyard came and stood beside me. "Why don't you take 'er grassin', Gaff?" A young man punched Gaff in the ribs and together they chased down the road.

Maggie is little and lively and twenty and she wants to see the world. She has never been farther than Sydney, a hundred miles away; in a few days she'll be leaving Neil's Harbour to get a job in Toronto. "I know I'll miss the salt water," she said, looking seaward, "and I'll make Mom and them all feel right bad, but the Harbour is always the same like, I don't want to stay here and git married and have babies every year while I wonder if my man will come home safe from fishin' like Mom done all her loife. I'm goin' to Toronto where there ain't no fishin'. I'm goin' real far away."

"Oh Maggie, ain't you scared?" Nellie asked.

"Sometimes," Maggie answered. "But I want to see Eaton's and Simpson's big stores, and moving pitchers, and go to dances in hotels with elevators."

"I guess you'll git nothin' but round dancin' in town," Nellie said wistfully.

"I loves round dancin'." Maggie merrily twirled in a dance step on the gravel road while a haunting voice came from the shadows, "Maggie dear, will you come with me?"

Maggie screeched, "Git on with ye, Charle, ye little beast, I'm not havin' no more to do with you."

CHAPTER FOURTEEN

SHIPWRECKS AND EARLY DAYS

WEDNESDAY, AUGUST 22

I ran over to Alec's this morning to ask him to tell me how Neil's Harbour began. "I lived in Cape North till I was raised," he said, "but old Reuben Swift was here from the beginning and he could tell you the best. Both him and his wife's blind and will be glad for someone to talk to; they're in that little house with no paint behind Matt Clipper's place."

At the back door I was welcomed by Mr. Swift, a thin grizzled man who looked like pictures of Vincent Van Gogh. Mrs. Swift, knitting by the kitchen window, turned a quiet face with clouded eyes towards me as I told them why I had come. "Ain't that fine, Mother? We'll be able to help her," Mr. Swift patted her hand and the old lady smiled. "Now, girlie, you sit on that chair right close to us and I'll tell you: I come from Newfoundland when I were eight year old and that were seventy year ago, my wife come when she were four months." He patted her again. "We had no children, Mother and I, we have no one of our own to look after us. I had a little money in the bank once but we used it all up long ago." The man's dim eyes looked fearful.

"You're going to tell her the history, Dad," his wife reminded.

"Oh yes, that's what she come for," Mr. Swift smiled again. "Well now here's how it was," he leaned towards me. "A long time ago a man named Neil McLeod lived near Ste. Anne's; he come up here fishing one summer by himself and went back home with such a great lot of mackerel and cod, people where he lived said, 'Next year let's all go up to Neil's Harbour to fish.' And that's how this place got its name and that's what started the Scotch people round Big Bras d'Or coming up here in 1868.

"Three or four families of men would come in a sailing vessel and bring provisions to last all summer. They didn't settle here, they had their farms and would come after the planting, they'd go home in August for hay-making and digging potatoes then come back and fish till Christmas. They lived in long log huts – barracks we called them – a row of them from the Point to where the Post Office is now. Six men would live in one building and they'd bring a daughter along to cook for 'em. They'd haul their big boats up on shore and fish in small ones. When they went home for the winter they'd leave the small boats in the huts and fill the big ones with fish."

"How did they keep the fish so long?" I wondered.

"They salted and dried them in sun till they were stiff as shingle, whole top of Point was covered with fish flakes in them days. I guess there's only a few up there now, have you noticed? Like long tables they are, covered with slats or chicken wire to lay the fish on."

"There are a few," I said, "but no fish on them."

"The fish boat collects now," he said. "Nothing's the same," he shook his head sadly, "everything's changing, I mind . . ."

"Tell her when we come," the old woman prompted him.

"Oh yes," he brightened. "We come from Rose Blanche, where her father and one other was the first settlers into it in 1808. Winter fishing were hard and dangerous along south shore of Newfoundland so in 1869 we come across the strait and settled

125

into the Cove; some went to Ingonish and in 1875 some from each place moved to Neil's Harbour. Newfoundlanders weren't like the Scotch, they were real fishermen, spent all their time fishing.

"A merchant always come and went back with the Scotch people, he owned all the land in the Cove so no other merchant could come in and trade. He were so pleased with us staying here that he sent over a vessel to Newfoundland to fetch more immigrants; the *Secret,* a ship with three sails, made several trips. Some of the families that came brought their houses with them; they took them apart, put them on her deck and when they landed here they put them together again."

"Are they still here, Dad?" Mrs. Swift asked.

"No dear, they fell down or was took down and new ones put up. Neil's Harbour were all Crown land and you could put your house wherever you liked. A man chose a piece of ground, put a fence around it and after he lived in it for thirty years it was better'n a grant."

"Could a person still do that?" I wondered.

"It ain't all Crown land now, some of it's been granted, but if you want to beat the goverment you could still put up a house. It wouldn't be so hard to do now there's a clearing. When we come the bush was right to the water and you had to cut it down to build. There was sixteen families here and twelve in the Cove, they cut down everything and burned it or used it for building till not a tree was left on the hill."

"Those first settlers didn't think about the look of the place," Mrs. Swift said.

"Why don't people plant trees now?"

"I couldn't say, we tried planting some round the house once or twice but cows come and et them."

"We lived here three years when we bought a cow," the old man continued, "before that the merchant had two cows and that's all there was, women had to nurse their children till they got their teeth. The Scotch people brought us butter and eggs till we hatched our own hens.

"The merchants used to send their vessels south full of fish and bring back cloth and gear from Halifax, but we had no money to buy it. Fish wasn't any price; in those days the merchants treated us like heathens, they'd take two quintals – that's three hundred pounds fish – for a box o' raisins. Lobster was fifty cents a hundred pound; I were high line but I couldn't make a living. We were so poor the goverment had to send in cornmeal and flour to keep us from starving." The old man crossed to a corner of the kitchen and drank from a dipper in a bucket, then returned wearily to his chair.

His wife told me calmly, "In those days everyone came and went in boats. There was no road, just a footpath through the woods between us and the other places and you'd have to stoop way down to get clear of the bushes. The postman would bring mail once a week on his back, except in winter.

"The first church was built here in 1878 and they started a school in a store loft. 1890 was the year of the fire: it started in July on the Ingonish road, crossed the blueberry barrens and came behind Neil's Harbour, burning the fences at Patsons. We all moved our belongings down to the Point and we camped there while the men fought the blaze till they saved all the houses. Rain came and the fire died down but it broke out again in September and so fierce that sparks came right across the harbour and started some sawdust at Calvin Leaf's sawmill. And it never stopped burning altogether till into October."

"That was a terrible anxious time," Mr. Swift started again. "The next year, 1891, I took the first census; 'twas about like it is now – 260 in Neil's Harbour and 250 in Cove. The popilation is always the same like – some gets born, some dies, and some gets out. I can tell you how many's been drowned: nine in New Haven and three in Harbour. Six got killed in the war, forty-two went over to it. There's been more turned out of here than is left. Sometimes a whole family with married children moves out, thinkin' they'll do better workin' in the Sydneys. And a good many went to sea."

"Did you ever go away?"

"Oh yes, I used to go on trips to Halifax and Boston. Once I went on a wrecking steamer for three months, they took me because I knowed where the wrecks was. There was an awful lot of them till the lighthouses was put up around the coast. All the big ships used to pass this way and a grand sight it was when windjammers and brigantines came sailing by. But sometimes

127

they would come too close to shore and go on rocks – a terrible thing to see 'em smashed to kindlin' wood. In 1869 the *Architect,* coming from Quebec with heavy squared timber, was wrecked near the schoolhouse. Five steamers I know of got wrecked just out there," he gestured towards the eastern shore, "but no lives lost.

"The *Ariadne,* a square rigger out of Norway, coming by in the night mistook Neil's Harbour Light for Money Point and went aground at Green Cove, just round them rocks across the beach, with all hands lost but two. Five of the bodies washed ashore and I asked the clergyman why they couldn't be put in burying ground here. He wired Halifax to ask the bishop's permission and a crowd of us fishermen made coffins out of pieces of wreck and buried them.

"The clergyman wrote to the Norway consul to tell him what we done and he told King Oscar back in Norway. The king asked the consul to find out what we wanted for our work and we said 'Nothin', we was glad to do it,' so King Oscar sent us a gold Communion cup, an awful expensive thing made of pure gold. If you go up to the rectory Mr. Nash will show it to you."

A young neighbour woman came in and started a fire to make the blind couple's dinner. "Come back again," they said as I was leaving. Mr. Swift added, "I'll think up more to tell you but if you want a real story about a wreck you ask Tom Candle about the *Caribou.*"

Tom Candle was alone in his stage when I asked him to tell me the story of the *Caribou.* "It happened to me," he said solemnly. "It happened when I were going to Newfoundland to see my father, eighty-four year old."

"Were you shipwrecked?"

"I were torpedoed!" Then I remembered that the *Caribou* was the passenger steamer sunk in the Cabot Strait by a Nazi submarine during the war. Tom said, "She never stayed up five minutes after she were hit. All the crew was drownded. I can't always tell about it, my throat gits filled up and it's no good."

He started talking in a strange, slow, halting way that had a sort of rhythm.

"Sydney I leaves at nine o'clock, on steamer *Caribou*.

I walked on deck all night, at four I went below.

I had no chance to git a belt when the torpedo struck." He broke off and looked at me, "You can make it rhyme when you write it down in the book." he said, then went on as if he were dictating.

"When torpedo struck I rushed on deck and got in lifeboat;
  Boat 'commodated fifty but seventy-five got in.

As we shoved away from side she up and overturned." Tom paused then went on more quickly in his natural voice. "To tell you the truth, my dear girl, I went under the water and when I come up I swimmed a dozen strokes right into a big body of men grabbing holt of each other like they was crazy; I had to go under water again to git clear of 'em. Just as I reached the lifeboat three gun shots was fired from the sub and *Caribou* disappeared."

As if in a trance, Tom continued slowly,
"I ketched holt of a girl and drawed her into boat.

The sea was awful rough and it were awful cold,

Submarine come under us and over we turned again;

The girl could not get clear and she poor thing were drowned." Glancing at me Tom said, "I forgot to tell you, first time boat went over I sung 'Jesus Pilot Me' and I wasn't nervous no more after that, seemed like I got new strength. They sung it in church for me too when I got home."

Tom's face resumed its strange look as he recited the epic experience of his life that only verse was great enough to express.
"Seventy-five was in our boat before torpedo struck,

When daylight come only five was left.

I seen a Canadian sailor as 'e let go his hold.

He had a life belt on and I grabbed onto it." Tom looked at me and went on normally. "I held sailor for hours and hours till corvette come alongside. They lashed us to the rescue boat and took three men off, one had a death grab so tight they could hardly git 'is hands clear. I was hangin' on to sailor and they couldn't git me off till I let go of him. I says to boatman, 'Haul in my sailor quick,' but sailor never kep' his face out o' water and when they got 'im aboard he was dead. I felt awful bad but I couldn't do no more. The water was too cold and I was shook up terrible."

129

Tom bent low over his net. "I only had five teeth on top but they all got knocked out on the trip; I got false ones now for Sundays, but that's nothin' to what some people went through in the war."

Tom looked up the road where a handsome stranger was steadying a young fisherman who was more than a little tipsy. Tom called, "Welcome Rorie, come and set you." The stranger shook Tom's hand, the drunken one gave me a pat as he passed me sitting on the ramp.

"Leave 'er alone, Johnnie," Tom said. "Where'd you git it?"

"Dingwall, lotsa boats in Dingwall." Johnnie almost tipped over a keg as he sat on it. With a sozzled smile he began to sing about a little yellow dory. Tom looked uneasy, the stranger muttered, "Shut up, Johnnie."

"Girl likes singin', don't you?" Johnnie lurched towards me.

"Save that one fer trawl baitin'," Tom growled.

"To hell with you," Johnnie reeled down the ramp and the stranger led him away. Tom and I watched them out of sight. "Now there's a nice feller for you, Rorie Macmillan from Sugarloaf. Got 'is arm hurt bad in war, wouldn't be able to beat ye; but 'e thinks 'e thinks 'e's awful pretty looking, that's what 'e do."

After supper I was sitting in an old rowboat drawn up on the stones near Molly's house. Jeanie, Sandy and Philip were in it too making sling shots from a piece of rubber tubing. Molly came out to us, "Philip, where's Arlie?"

"Don't know, never seen 'im."

"That keed, we ain't seen en since breakfast. Sayed 'e were goin' to Weeyam's [William's] ower in Cove but Willie says 'e ain't there and wasn't." An anxious look crossed Molly's face. "Could ha' slipped in ower them rocks by east shore," she said uneasily, then shrugged her shoulders. "Well if 'e did there's no use lookin' for 'im now, 'e's drownded sure and good by this toime. I'm supprised when noight comes and they's all safe in bed." The little girls clung to her skirt. "Let go me," she shrieked and they loosened their hold but kept looking up at her. She said quietly, "Guess Oi better go off and try an' foind en."

"Could I go for you?"

"No, you wouldn't know where to look, but come with me.

Philip you watch Sandy, don't let 'er go on wharf. We got go foind Arlie." We started down the road between the stages. The children followed. Molly turned on Philip, furious with fear, "You leetle son of a beetch, didn't Oi tell you to stay there and watch Sandy? Now do as Oi tells ye."

The children retreated, we went on. We hadn't gone far when Arlie came towards us; small, dirty and frightened as Molly screamed, "Arlie, you booger, where you been at all day? Get on oop there to the house, Fred's goin' beat you and beat you good when he gits hold o' you." Arlie ran, giving us a wide margin.

Molly mused, "Now where d'you think 'e were all day?" She called to the little boy. "Did you 'ave anything to eat?" Arlie nodded but soon after I saw him munching a chunk of bread as he walked briskly from the house to the little outhouse in the corner of the yard, singing to himself in his innocent boyish soprano, "I eats and I eats and I eats; I shits and I shits and I shits; I eats and I eats and I eats; I shi ..." The outhouse door slammed shut.

I was on my way to the house to put on warmer clothes when Rorie Macmillan came along the road with Jossie. "Going to the Co-op show at the Hall?" he asked me. "Walk along with us." He looked like a Viking; the handsomest man I've seen in Cape Breton. I fell into step. But he talked only to Jossie and when we reached the Hall he was surrounded by welcoming friends and forgot that I existed.

"It's cold, do you think I have time to run home for a jacket?" I asked Tom Candle, who was standing near me.

"Yes, ye better, there's measles around might git you."

People were strolling to the Hall from both villages and when I got back it was so crowded that I was barely able to squeeze inside the doorway, but somehow Rorie was able to squeeze in beside me.

Three strange men who had set up a screen, movie projector and a heavy gasoline motor were sitting on the platform. One of the visitors introduced the others then extolled work done by the Co-operative movement in Nova Scotia. He told of the benefits enjoyed by fishermen who had organized a society and shared the profits formerly made by the buyers alone. "You fishermen think you are independent because you run your own boats, but you are completely at the mercy of the buyer who takes your fish to the city market and pays you a pittance. It's a crying shame there's no electricity along this coast," he shouted. "There is no reason why people in Neil's Harbour and New Haven must live in ignorance, poverty and isolation." The audience listened quietly but as he went on the young people around me were saying, "What's he talkin' for?" "Can't understand 'im." "Thought we was goin' to have a show." "Shshshshshshshshsh-shsh . . ."

When it was dark enough for the pictures the gasoline engine roared. The first film showed statistical diagrams and pictures of Co-op executives attending a conference; the next film, a travelogue of Scotland, made everyone roar with laughter; the third picture, of Gaspé fishermen, inspired interested comment: "Look at them old two-stemmers they's usin'." "Must be awful backward on Gaspé." "Good thing we's livin' here where we's better off."

When the entertainment was over the handsome stranger put his good arm through mine and walked me down the road in the moonlight. I was thinking there is no darkness in the Harbour, there is only sunlight and moonlight, when a little voice warned, "Be careful Aidna, 'e's got lots o' girls."

CHAPTER FIFTEEN

POLITICS DON'T CARE FOR WE

THURSDAY, AUGUST 23

After the films and rousing speeches in the Hall last night I was surprised to find the men in Tom Candle's stage strangely apathetic this morning. "I thought everybody would be excited today about organizing a Co-operative Society," I said.

"No, nothin' like that," drawled Leo Budge, a wiry little man on the table. "We ain't much fer politics."

"Don't you get worked up over elections?"

"We just goes and votes, all very quiet." Tom was mending a net. "We votes different every time, we always thinks maybe a change would be better."

"Politics in now ain't never done nothin' for us," said Black Bert, a man with a dark whiskery face.

"They give us that gasoline engine for haulin' boats," Tom said.

"They give us that instead of a harbour," said Bert angrily.

"Every morning, October to January, we gits up at five and launches boats, and at night we hauls 'em up again, and after we hauls 'em we still got to bait our trawls for next day. Can't get to bed till we's wore out."

Tom said, "We needs a harbour bad; could dig through sand beach and dredge out sand and we'd have it."

"Don't think we'll ever git it," Leo said.

"They comes round and measures the water every few years," Tom told us.

"They don't need to come round wi' their measurin' sticks, water's always the same," the dark man spat. "They just wants votes, they never does nothing."

"We only wants harbour big enough for our own," Tom explained to me. "We don't want none o' them big company boats cuttin' through our nets, breakin' our trawls and takin' our fish; some has as many as fourteen dories to 'em, fishin' day and night, can store their fish aboard and take rough water. We don't want them in here."

Big Jim Clipper said, "Seems like politics don't care for we."

"You're right," Leo said. "A few years ago when depression were on we peoples was pretty poor off, we had to wheel all our fish down to Cove in a barrow and make a trade with the merchant. He give us tea or sugar – or whatever – and if we had a little over from the trade he give us credit, never no money."

"You couldn't have what you wanted neither," Jim said, opening the blade of a jack-knife, "them with big families was on relief and if they got sugar they couldn't git molasses, they only let 'em have certain things that was just enough to live on, no coffee or nothing that was a luxury."

"That's horrible, ain't it?" Black Bert looked mad. "Hundred pound o' fish weren't enough for a pound o' tea. Luke Buffet had thousand pound haddick and all 'e got for 'em was a haxe."

"If anyone maked two hunnert credit for a whole year's fishin' they was good off – and there was plenty o' fish," Leo said.

"We can't have that kind o' thing goin' on no more," Jim Clipper's ruddy face was grim. "If politics in now . . ."

"Shhhh. . .," Tom Candle warned. "Here's Doctor." A young man wearing a white shirt leaned out of his car and asked Tom if his salt herring was ready to be picked up.

134

"Yes sir, this afternoon, and I'll tell you now, sir, don't put no fresh water with it, one teaspoon would spoil the whole pickle.'

When the doctor drove on Tom said, "Nice man, that, and 'e can pull teeth too."

"'e never pulled your's, Tom," Leo said.

"No, I often wonders where them got to, don't know if I swallered 'em or if they's down on the bottom."

Alf Clipper was in Tom Candle's stage after dinner; he'd been swordfishing in the morning and found it very rough. His boy was scared but Alf said he didn't care, he'd keep going out as long as he could stay in the rigging.

When he left us Tom leaned towards me, confidentially, "Now that man is right foolish, sayin' 'e's goin' out there when it's rough as this – ye got a long time daid. Ye might as well take good care o' yourself while you're alive. I'd rather go pickin' blueberries on a day like this, but you know that feller's awful fer the money; and what good is it goin' do him if he's drownded?"

Tom looked at me over his glasses and pointed his shuttle. "Of course you know they say Tom Candle's foolish; 'e don't do like rest of fellers, 'e goes 'is own way. You don't see the rest of 'em mendin' naits, do ye? No, they's sittin' round somewheres playin' poker. They waits till it's near time to put nait out in water then they's in a hurry, rushin' here and rushin' there and complainin' they's got too much to do and I can take me time. Then they says, 'It's all right fer you, you got yours done, but we's got t' do ours.'"

Tom stretched his net, looking for holes. "Some don't bother much atall. They puts 'em out the way they is, full o' holes. That's a terrible thing, you know, terrible, terrible, terrible. Not takin' care of a nait is a sin. One time ye could git a good nait fer thirteen or fifteen dollars, now they's up to forty. Well that's a lot o' money. I take good care o' mine; ye see that barrel there? That's where I puts 'em, keeps 'em good and dry. I got some I had for twenty-three year, some round 'ere buys new ones every four year. Then they never got no money. I ain't got much but I never need a lick o' help from nobody and I don't want it; I weren't on relief in the depression." Tom spat. "I paid my way."

"You seen lots of people round 'ere is gettin' them new parlour sets from the catalogue. I'm not. Me and wife's gettin' old and might git sick and I'd rather 'ave the money laid by to pay fer it if I have to instead o' spendin' every cent I got. We has a nice home the way it is." Tom deftly mended a hole.

"And another thing, you seen how people is round 'ere on Sunday, always puttin' on their good clothes and settin' around. Well I used to do that but not any more. Afore you know it yer helpin' haul up a boat or something, ye haven't time to run home and change and ye spoils yer good things. Now I just wears me old ones on Sunday. Got a good suit at home, tailor made four years ago and only had it on twice."

Tom looked at me sharply. "Now don't git me wrong, I ain't stingy; I always believed in 'love yer neighbour as yerself' and if I can do a good turn to somebody I does it. Course I ain't too good," he grinned, "times I's right wicked."

"How?"

"Oh words, I gits mad quick and says words I shouldn't say, like everybody do, but if I can help anybody I does it. Maybe you seen that Hindian was round 'ere last week with baskets? 'e had no place to stay and asked if 'e could stay with we; 'e said nobody'd 'ave 'im cause 'e was a Hindian. Well I wouldn't let the pore feller stay outside so we kep' 'im for couple nights and feeded 'im, 'tain't 'is fault 'e was born a Hindian."

My mail came at four o'clock; I dashed with it to my room and read and reread for an hour. One letter told about a dance at the golf club, another was gossipy, a couple had invitations; my male relatives will be greatly disappointed if I don't catch a swordfish; my mother's letter showed concern about my interest in fishermen and told me she has seen George calling quite often next door where a pretty girl from Regina is visiting.

I wonder if I could be happy here without the secure knowledge that I have friends waiting for me to come back to them. The letters have made me restless. They have recalled things at home that I greatly enjoy but have momentarily forgotten; I've become so engrossed in Neil's Harbour and the ways of its people that not much else seems important or real.

Yet here I am often lonely. But my loneliness is poignant only at nightfall when people walk along the road together and lights in the houses suggest friendly company. Tonight as I sat on my fence rail with the sea moving near me, the setting sun tinting the windy sweep of clouds over the Light, I longed for someone with whom I could share the wild beauty.

Big Jim Clipper, wearing a navy turtleneck sweater under a faded olive pullover with sleeves cut off at the elbows, came down the road towards me. "Do you ever think how beautiful it is here?" I asked him when he leaned against the fence.

"Guess not," he grinned, "Oi just looks and Oi thinks, 'Is she goin' to blow or ain't she goin' to blow?'"

Old John Clipper came limping along with his cane, his cap rakishly on one side of his head. "You always writin', ain't you?" he said. "Must be noice to write," he looked wistfully at my notebook. "Never could figure out how people done it." He examined a page. "All them little marks got meanin' to 'em ain't they?" he said. "Hit's a funny thing," he raised his cap and scratched his scalp, "first they's in your haid, then you puts 'em on paper, someone else sees 'em and if they can read they gits 'em in their haid. That way anybody can git same thing you got." Old John nodded, limped away slowly, then turned to call back to me, "Guess people needs be awful perticler what they writes."

Matt Clipper came along next. "Here ye are, settin' again," he said, opening his knife to whittle the rail. "What you want to know about this toime?" he smiled.

I asked about the government of the village. The thought puzzled him. "Oi don't roightly know what you mean, ain't nobody's no more'n nobody else, we all just runs our own show." He paused to think. "Or do you mean something loike school trustees? We got three o' them for gettin' teachers and lookin' after the buildin' and that: Mrs. Mackay in Cove, Jack Seaforth and me." He frowned, "This year we can't git no teachers nohow, we's in an awful pickle. Old people round 'ere don't care, they never had much chance for schoolin', but us young ones be gettin' more for eddication, specially for the women. A girl usually gits married round seventeen but if she can figger and write good she can help her man git ahead more." Matt held up his great work-gnarled hands, "These is too big for handlin' little small pencils, they's better for fishin' and buildin'." He laughed.

137

"Buildin' is what Oi loikes, when everyone's workin' together. We built Hall in three days. School and churches taked longer. Have you been inside churches?"

"Not yet, but I like the outside of both of them, and the Anglican graveyard sloping down to the sea."

Matt looked at me curiously, his head on one side. "You really loike it here, don't you?"

"I love it."

Matt said, "Men was sayin' the other day seems just loike you be one of us."

I had to turn my head to hide my grateful tears.

CHAPTER SIXTEEN

MAGGIE'S LEAVING HOME

FRIDAY, AUGUST 24

The sputtering of a motor broke the night time stillness; beyond the Point there was a faint promise of light. I fumbled into my clothes, then ran to the shore where black figures were moving in the deep blue space that was the bay. A dory was being rowed towards the collar. "Take me, take me," I shouted. The starting roar of an engine swallowed my voice. I ran out to the end of the fishdock and shouted again. My only answer was the blat of another motor as the men in the dory, transferred to their larger craft, were on their way to the sea.

And that was that. Codfishing be damned. I shivered in the misty air. Nothing to do but go back to bed.

Then I saw something move in one of the anchored boats. Or did I? The light was very dim, I strained my eyes in the blueness. For a moment only I distinctly saw a form. Wearing a hat: that meant Mr. Battersey. I shouted. He went down. He came up. I called again. He went down again and stayed down.

I scanned the shore in hope of another prospect. Near the stages was a short bent man: Tom Candle. "Up awful early, ain't you?" he said when I reached him.

"I want to go codfishing."

"Wouldn't none of 'em take ye?"

"I was too late and Mr. Battersey seems to be having trouble with his motor."

"He often do, he's seventy-four year old and just can't understand 'em. Never got used to 'em."

We watched the antics of the black fedora then Tom said, "Pore old George. You know 'e were tellin' me last night 'e'd like right well to take ye out fishhin'."

"Then why doesn't he? Everybody tells me they'd like to but nobody does it."

Tom bent his head and looked at me steadily over his glasses, "Now me and you's friends, ain't we?"

"Of course."

"Then you won't git fashed if I tell you straight out why it is?"

"I want to know."

He rubbed the back of his neck. "Well, I'm a married man so I guess it's all right for me to say it," he hesitated, "you see, hit's like this: men fishin' cod in summer is mostly old like George Batt'sey," he shifted to look at the water instead of at me, "'tain't same as with young ones, old fellas is weaker like and," he kicked at a stone, "and when they gits out there in them small boats, they – well – now and again they's got to stop and – GO!"

"So that's it?" I laughed.

Tom looked at me with relief, "Yes, that's all 'tis, it ain't nothin' against you."

"I'm so glad."

"Pore George, 'e felt right bad last night." Tom was looking at the boats. "Where is 'e now? Never falled owerboard did 'e? Oh no, there 'e is, there's 'is wite haid, 'e's tooked off 'is hat. 'e'll never git fishin' today." We watched Mr. Battersey floating around, then Tom said, "Got go up now and git my boy out for swordfishin'."

I looked at him hopefully, "Maybe I could go swordfishing?"

"I got only small boat," he grinned. "Forecast said a sou'easter is bringin' dirty weather and all snapper boats but one has gone off to Dingwall and that one will have to put in too."

"I wouldn't mind, I wouldn't mind going in at Dingwall."

Tom again solemnly explained the facts of life. "It wouldn't be right for ye to go with 'em when they ties up and sleeps in the fo'c'sle."

"Of course not, but couldn't I get a ride back?"

Tom shook his head as he hitched up his braces, "Now you tell me one thing," he looked at me over his glasses, "maybe you noticed that Neil's Harbour men is fine fellers?"

"I surely have."

"Well in Dingwall right now they's three hundred boats from far away and all over. Neil's Harbour men wouldn't take a lady in there because some o' them men be right brazen."

On my way back to the house I met Maggie Patson coming off night duty at the hospital where for a year she's been nurses' aiding and cooking and saving her earnings to leave a life that is tranquil and sure for one that is startling and new. "That's my last night working in there," Maggie said gaily, "soon I'll be earning eighty dollars a month in the city. And every week I'll send home a present for somebody." (The hospital's twelve-hour duty is strenuous, allowing six half days off in a month that pays fifty-eight dollars. It is the only work available for a girl who lives in Neil's Harbour – except a job at eighteen cents an hour cleaning lobster in season, or doing housework for a dollar a day.)

"Come home with me and see me off," Maggie invited, and I happily walked along with her.

Maggie is the fifth youngest of her mother's thirteen children. Bill, Pete, Fred, Bobbie and Jean have homes of their own in the village; Annie and her family live in Sydney Mines; Mary in Glace Bay; Eva and her husband and baby have rooms in Toronto; and Norman's away in the army. The rest of the Patsons live in the brown shingle house on the hill.

When we arrive Wesley, Maggie's father, is codfishing; Stuart is eating breakfast; Gordie is milking the freckle-rumped cow; Dolly is playing with a cousin near the woodpile; Philip reluctantly carries water from the brook. In the kitchen on the lounge beside the stove, plump little Abe Budge, eighty-one, from next door, is smoking his pipe; Jean and her baby come for a pickle jar of milk. I sit unnoticed on a chair near the door. Above the whir of the gasoline-operated washing machine, Ella Jane, Maggie's mother, screams, "Look at Stuart's shirt, his best one put it on and went and lanched a boat, now it's roight beat up. Maggie, go darn these socks, they got as many holes into 'em as a herrin' net."

Maggie tosses the socks into the air. "Not me, Mom, soon I'll be goin' on a train for two days and two nights."

"Uh, uh," grunts the old man on the lounge, "it's a long ride fer yer first one."

"I'm goin' to stay awake all the way so I won't miss none o' the sights." Maggie snatches the striped denim cap off old Abe's head, puts it on her own and pretends she is engineering. "Choo-choo, Dolly, watch out or I'll run over you and the cat." She peers out of an imagined cab. "I wants to see what it's like when we leaves Cape Breton and crosses over to Nova Scotia."

Maggie is merry and mad and impulsive, wherever she is there is laughter. Her restless *joie de vivre* can't be sustained in Neil's Harbour. She turns on the radio to a Cape Breton station that plays old time music. "You got the money and I got the time," she sings and step dances, puts on a man's jacket and waves its long sleeves like a scarecrow.

"Maggie, don't be so foolish," her mother calls, "git to Jesus on upstairs and paint the sill in the boarder's bedroom. I've riz up the window and took down the curtain."

As Maggie obeys she wistfully says, "It will be some strange to live in a small room by myself, in a house with no space a-round it."

The Patsons' house in the centre of its rocky field has eight rooms, but everyone likes to gather in the enormous kitchen to be with Ella Jane, whose heart is as warm and crackling with affection as the fire that burns in the shiny black stove. There is always someone sitting on the rocker or the wooden lounge built into the corner, always a grandchild hoping for a cookie, always a neighbour on the chair beside the door of the closed porch where the waterpails and rubber boots are kept. The kitchen looks like a baby clinic when the young mothers come with their little ones to call for their daily pint.

"In town all you need do is put a ticket in a bottle outside your door and a man brings your milk," Maggie tells them.

"For all that, I wouldn't want to do without my old cow," Ella Jane says, "she's the koindest cow I ever had. Wesley's got to sharpen the scythe and make hay for her one o' these days."

"Eva wrote I better git Dad to cobble my shoes that needs it before I go," Maggie says.

"I guess you won't find a man so handy as him in town," Ella Jane observes dryly as Wesley shambles in, carrying a codfish by the tail. Like most men at Neil's Harbour, Wesley can do almost anything. "But if that man knows there's a hair cuttin' to do he'd do it 'stead of earnin', he's that crazy for it," Ella Jane declares. In the Patson kitchen, the yard or the cow-barn – wherever is most convenient – Wesley safety-pins the back slit of an old khaki coat round the neck of whoever comes for a clipping. His skill in the barberless village has a reputation. "He never finished Reid's hair though," Ella Jane says. "Got one side done and stopped to emp' the pail of slops under the sink and the child hasn't let him git handy to him since. Wesley's give him lime juice and tatie chips but he won't let him near with the scissor; he's been runnin' round fer a week now with 'is head just half cut."

"I might learn hair dressing," Maggie speculates. "They pay money for a hair cut in town."

"You better stick to housework," Ella Jane advises. "That's what you knows how to do."

Maggie scowls, "I'd rather go in a factory, you don't got to work so long."

"Work won't hurt you, you'll never git sick while you've something to do and someone to do for," says Ella Jane, whose work for her family is never done. "You might git a job bakin' bread," she suggests, "that baker's stuff from town don't seem to last no time inside the men when they's out on the water. Gordie, git me some chips, there ain't a livin' spark in the stove."

"Soon I'll just have to sit in a restaurant and order whatever I want." Maggie lights a cigarette like a grande dame. "I'm goin' to tell 'em my name is Marguerite," she says impishly, "or should I change it to Bernadette?"

"Oh Maggie, don't talk so foolish, I don't know how we'll git on without you," her mother laments.

A twinge crosses Maggie's face. "I'll make lots o' money and send Dolly a dress and I'll get ties for Stuart and Dad straight out of Eaton's." Maggie dances around the room. "And I'll buy myself a formal and go to a New Year's Ball in a big high building like we seen in the pitchers in Sydney."

"You'll git lonesome when you ain't handy to home," Stuart tells her as he pulls on his rubber boots.

"No I won't. Eva and Richard and others from the Harbour's up there, there's lots o' Cape Bretoners in Toronto, they has a dance for 'em every month. Why don't you come too, Stuart? We could git a place together."

Stuart shakes his head. "I'd rather stay where I'm at and go fishin'."

Maggie grabs him and they swing to the radio's country music. Gordie swings Dolly, Ella Jane swings Philip and they all laugh with breathless delight.

"Truck goin' ower to Dingwall tonight fer a dance," says the stout old man from next door.

Ella Jane protests, "They can't spend money fer that, they got just as good Times in their own place. Bobby Clipper plays the guitar loud as any and Herman's right smart on the fiddle."

"But I loves to drive in a car," Maggie's eyes are glowing. "When I gets up there to Ontario maybe I'll git some rides; everybody there's got cars."

Though all the fishermen own or share a boat with a car motor, none of them have a car. When there is a dance in Ingonish or Dingwall the young people pay a dollar a trip to ride in the back of a truck.

"You goin' to dance, Abe?" Maggie asks the old man.

He looks surprised and says, "If my laigs wasn't so bad I'd take you. Ain't been to a dance in seventy year."

Stuart says, "You was too, you ain't that old. I'm only twenty-three and I remembers the time you fell over the bank behind Pride's."

The old man uncomfortably rubs his hand across his long yellowed moustache and shakes his head. "No, no, not me."

"Yis you did too," Stuart persists, "I seen you."

Wesley, blissfully riding Dolly and a grandchild on the rocker, said, "They had to haul 'im up with a rope."

Stuart goes on, "You ain't so old or so bad off as you makes out, you's just as smart as we is if you wants to be. If you had a quart o' rum in you you'd be good at a dance as ever you was."

"He's too fat," Dolly declares.

"You thinks I's fat, but I ain't, I's swole." The old man gets up indignantly and stomps out of the house.

"Stuart, you shouldn't tease the pore old soul," Ella Jane says fondly. "It's a sin, that's what it is, it's a sin."

Wesley grins, "Did you see the bottle sticking out his back pocket?"

Two brand-new travelling bags labelled Toronto are waiting in the Patsons' front room. Wesley, sipping his tea in the kitchen, says, "It was quite a family when all thirteen was at home. We used to need twelve barrels of flour in a year, now we'll only need four."

"Stuart thinks Maggie will be home again, don't you Stuart?" Ella Jane asks hopefully.

"Lots went away and came back," Stuart consoles her.

"I won't till I got a car," says Maggie, "unless I come home for Christmas."

Getting up and looking at the sea Stuart says, "It blows harder outside than it does in handy."

"I ain't scared," Maggie's eyes are brightly excited.

Stuart puts on his swordfishing cap and walks to the door. "Well, so long," he says to the sister he loves best of anyone in the world.

"So long," says Maggie.

Ella Jane shouts, "Maggie you eat something, do you want to starve to death on the way?"

Maggie asks quickly, "You goin' to shore now too, Gordie?"

"Yes, so long."

"So long."

Ella Jane's eyes fill with tears and she stays by the front room window as Wesley and Philip and Jean go down the hill to the bus that will carry Maggie away.

When Wesley came back to the house he shivered and said, "It seems just like a Fall day, don't it?" And Stuart when he came said the same.

CHAPTER SEVENTEEN

PIRATE GOLD

SATURDAY, AUGUST 25

Close to the eastern horizon soft folds of cloud were shaded with purple, saffron and slate; through narrow slits the rising sun made paths to the water; fishing boats crossed the spots of gleam like phantom silhouettes; the sky overhead was the blue of heavenly morning glories; coming swiftly from the mountains tattered masses of mist joined clouds above that were gold.

Alone on the Point I was both joyous and sad. I longed to hold the moment forever, to rouse everyone in the village to share it, I wanted all the world to exult in the beauty; at the same time I knew the splendour was fleeting and there would be no splendour at all in my street in the city. As I watched, the mists dissolved, the deep blue above grew paler, the colours on the line of the sea faded to grey as the clouds spread over the sky.

"Noice foine day," Matt Clipper called as we passed on my way home for breakfast, "Gonna have a squall o' rain and we needs it."

Several cars drove out to the Light and disgorged families of tourists who wandered all over the Point. Instead of greeting them like mates – as I did when I came here – I now stare at them or ignore them as the natives do, but I haven't acquired the fishermen's trick of spitting tobacco juice perilously close to a pair of open-toed sandals.

I found a sheltered spot by the shore and sat on a driftwood log, the creamy bones of codfish scattered near it. I've forgotten how upholstery feels; I'm patterned by rocks, docks, fence rails and crowberry bushes.

Molly's little girls and the Clipper twins, Louise and Lily, were soon around me. Gwendoline's dress was splattered with paint that she kept trying to hide. Jeanie was making a bird's nest. When she left it to collect more grass Louise stole it away and hid it under my jacket; when Jeanie couldn't find it she told us she'd thrown it overboard, and made another nest. Lily sneaked it away again. Jeanie was mystified when she came back with a handful of straw, "I never really trowed it overboard, I only said I did."

"A big black bird came and got it," Lily giggled. When Jeanie was gone again Lily formed the grass into a nest and put a pebble in it which Jeanie delightedly believed was an egg.

We saw a ship coming our way and ran to the wharf to watch: it was the government lightship bringing kerosene to the Light; two boats came ashore with twelve men to land a drum of coal oil and a broom.

By mid-morning the sea had changed its blue to grey with spreading white wings and the rain was pelting. Swordfishing boats sailed into the Harbour, drenched men swaying on their masts; codfishermen gutted their catch in gleaming oilskins and sou' westers; women set out pails and barrels to catch the precious water; dripping children splashed in puddles. Disgruntled tourists sat in their cars while the wind blew gusts against their closed windows.

I ran for shelter to a stage where Matt Clipper and a dressed-up old stranger were standing in the doorway. The man was pointing to the wall of rock on the far side of the bay. "You see that deep cut? Well George Batt'sey and me was over there one Sunday just looking around and we found a new shovel and crowbar lyin' on ground by a deep hole so we put 'em in it and breaked off a branch so we'd know where to find 'em.

"We wanted to go back next day but thought we better wait till it was thick-a-fog and nobody'd see us. We told Jim Clipper about it but 'e said 'e don't want nothing to do with it. Three weeks after me and George went over again." The man's mouth opened to enact surprise. "Crowbar and shovel was gone! Yes sir, we trampled all the growth round the hole but couldn't find nothing so we had to come back because we got nothing to dig with.

"Couple days later Jim says 'e gotta git juniper for spar on 'is boat and 'e'd take me with 'im. We went to the hole: crowbar and shovel was there! Jim gits 'is juniper but wouldn't do no digging and taked shovel home with 'im. I had a hoe I brought with me so I leaved it and crowbar in hole.

" 'nother week George and me goes over again and this time hoe and crowbar is gone! So we gives up. That were twenty year ago and I moved away from Harbour soon after that. But I'm going over there again before I leave this time."

"What's over there?" I asked.

Matt answered. "There's supposed to be money buried. One o' them pirates put it there years and years ago. They say 'e had a great lot o' gold and killed all 'is crew but one, between the two of 'em they buried it and people's been diggin' all over Cape Breton ever since."

"And it ain't found yet," the old man said. "Feller at Whoite Point said a stranger on road seemed to lead 'im to a place then disappeared in the air! He dug and something pressed down on him so 'e could hardly rise up but 'e couldn't see nothing. He was never right in the head after that."

"Terrible, ain't it?" Matt said. "Feller 'ere dreamed a man come to 'im one noight and told 'im place to dig; next day 'e got in boat and went over to the high rock. Soon as 'e started diggin' all the bushes and alders fell flat loike they was bowin'! 'e got that scared 'e just run, 'e didn't want to see no man walkin' round with no head on loike they doos when they's guardin' treasure."

After dinner Calvin Leaf came to the house to get a jar of milk. "I got five cats now I's feedin' but I only wants milk for one, the big he-cat. 'e must'a got in a foight. 'e's hurt roight bad, don't go nowhere, just sets all day alongside of I."

"Has he been eating?" I asked.

"Not much, I thought milk moight be good fer 'e. I gived 'e cod's tongues, got no bones hinto 'em, 'e loikes 'em, but 'e wouldn't 'ave 'em so I cooked 'em fer meself. Not often I has fish, guess I only 'ad fish four toimes this year; too much trouble to clean it and cook it."

"What do you eat, Calvin?" Katie asked.

"Oh I gits pork chops and sausingers, ain't no trouble to 'em, ye just puts in pan and cooks 'em fer a few minutes and they's done." Calvin paid for the milk and went out into the storm.

The rain was coming in waves; the sea was spraying over the breakwater, pounding on the stony shore; the boats were hauled from the water; wind ripped at the men's shiny oilskins; children ran with wet heads sleek as seals.

Alec's store was a friendly refuge. At mail time a little crowd had gathered in the space between the counters. There were puddles round the men's boots, water dripped from the children's hair.

"You still lookin' fer stories?" Big Jim Clipper asked me in his falsetto. "Better git George Batt'sey to tell you about 'is life and you'll have enough to fill your book. He'll tell you such yarns you'll have to walk away from 'im."

"He wants to go back to Heart's Content where 'e come from," Jack Seaforth spoke, "says he's goin' walk around fer a few days, not tell nobody who he is, let 'em guess."

"Whoi 'e's seventy-four year old and were only six when he left Newfoundland, nobody'd know 'im up there now, and nobody'd care fer the pore old feller," Matt said.

"Git him to tell you about fishin' at Whoite Point with old Diddle," Jim said to me. "A screecher come up, sea went woild, boat broke to kindlin' wood but Batt'sey got floated clean ashore, not even wet!"

"You should hear 'im tell about time 'e was courtin' his old woman and fell off fence on back of a bear," Jack laughed, "straddled it till 'e got knocked off in raspberry bushes."

"And about grandfather clock in Heart's Content that feller

used to keep 'is cow hinto all winter?" Big Jim doubled up with the titters.

"One time Batt'sey were travelling in the Boston States and, they told 'im there's a fire in the next town. Train started up so fast it went right out from under 'im and 'e had to run a hundred miles an hour to catch up to back of it," Jack Seaforth told.

"'ave 'im tell you about the big snow in Sydney when they drove the horses roight over the roof tops," Jim sputtered. "Oi don't know whoi he tells them lies, 'e's a good chap and would do anything for you."

The laughter subsided. Black Bert came into the store. "Well, Alec, what you got for me today? Yesterday I come down to git currants, they was maggotty, got a pound o' lamb: all bone, got taties: just like gum and roight black, got raisin bread: had only one raisin hinto it." He winked at Matt. "If you'd seen stuff 'e sent up there to 'ouse this morning with that young girl o' mine you couldn't feed it to a dog." Alec, sorting mail, glanced round the partition with a grin.

As we watched the rain lashing five horses gathered in front of the store, Bert said to a little boy beside him, "You watch a horse, 'e always stands ars to weather, that's himportant information to know."

A car scattered the animals and a young couple dashed for the store. We stared as they stood in our midst. The man asked, "Can we get fresh fruit here?" Matt Clipper told him no.

"How about soda biscuits?" One of the children jumped to the platform, ran behind the show case and taking a box from a shelf, tossed it to the tourist; Matt held out his hand for the money and gave it to Jim who reached it round the partition to Alec.

"Have you any fresh tomatoes?" the girl asked.

"Don't think," Matt said.

"Got some up to Dowling's," Jack muttered, "come on *Aspy* yestaday."

I didn't wait to hear more. I shoved myself through the deluge. There was exultation in the roar of the wind, wild waves reached greedily for the edges of the road where high-flung spray fell with the gimletting rain; rising grey sea and falling grey sky merged without a horizon. The earth drank like a sponge.

The tourist car passed me coming and going before I had

walked the half mile to the shop perched on the edge of the bank. With streams of water running from my slicker, I was blown through the doorway. The man behind the counter, round and rosy as Santa Claus, gave me four of his best tomatoes for a dime. "I'm glad they're such a treat," he said as I started to eat one. "People here don't care much for 'em, ain't used to 'em."

Near the store was the box-shaped mustard-coloured rectory where blind Reuben Swift had told me I should see the gift of the King of Norway. The rector welcomed me, brought out the precious little chalice and showed me a clipping from an old Halifax newspaper. "Presented to the Rev. Smith by the King of Sweden and Norway for an act of heroism. A Norwegian bark, the *Ariadne* of Sonsburg went to pieces in a storm off the coast of Cape Breton, October 7, 1896. The Rev. Smith, regardless of his own safety, put out in a small rowboat after the wrecked mariners and succeeded in bringing five of the drowned seamen to land and afterwards gave them Christian burial in the church-yard.

"The king, hearing of the noble work accomplished by the worthy rector, forwarded him the communion set. The chalice is of pure gold and beautifully enamelled in white and purple, the base set with pearls. On it is engraved, 'Rev. Atkinson Smith, Aedel Daad,' which means 'For a noble deed.' On the reverse side appears the crest of the king."

The clergyman talked to me for an hour about the people of his parish: "The finest I've ever worked with," his eyes glowed. "The men are known to be the best and bravest fishermen on the eastern coast. When you live with them you know why Christ chose fishermen to be his disciples: there are no egotists among them, the sea is their constant reminder of a Power greater than themselves." He smiled, "Of course I may idealize: they lack education and they do have their faults."

As I walked back along the road in rain that had become just a drizzle, I watched homely Sam Hatch, drenched and muddy, weaving drunkenly ahead of me: he'd teeter, get his balance, step forward carefully, lurch and almost fall. At the turn of the road near the Malcolms' he lunged then disappeared. When I came to the place where he'd been I saw him lying in water and grass in the ditch. "Would you find my keys for me please?" he asked.

"I dropped them somewheres there on the road and I can't find them."

They were in the mud almost beside me. I picked them up and gave Sam a hand out of the ditch. He clung pathetically. "Thank you, thank you very much," he said, "I'd like to put my arms round you and give you a kiss." As I backed away he hastened to add, "Now don't git me wrong, I'm not looking for t'rills, You know what I mean by t'rills? I mean sex, that's what I mean, SEX! I'm not looking for that. I want a woman, not for t'rills, but for clean shirts and darned socks."

"Of course I got sex," he almost shouted, "I got lots of sex. Not brutal, you know, just natural. Manly." He squared his narrow shoulders and swayed slightly. "I like a woman now and again, I had one last week, spent a whole night with her and it was – it was just like opening the gates to the Garden of Eden; a married woman she was who'd run out on her husband, said she was high sexed and she wanted some t'rills." He grinned and rolled his eyes. "Well, we had 'em."

Sam leaned against the Malcolms' fence. "It seems t'rills is all the girls are looking for nowdays. I want more than that. I want clean shirts and square meals. I want someone to keep my house nice like my mother used to do – God rest her soul – I had a wonderful mother; that's why I never married, I devoted myself to her, but last year she passed on at eighty-four and left me lonely. I haven't got anyone now, not a friend." Sam pulled out a dirty hankie.

"You're the only one I can talk to." He lowered his voice, "If you was so minded I'd go after you." As he lurched towards me I stepped back. "No, I thought not," he drooped, "you wouldn't have the likes of me. But you ain't the only fish in the sea. I'm fifty-four year old and I got a girl young as you are who'd take me if I asked her to. 'Sammie,' she says, 'you're sweet.' That's what she says.

"I bring her things, nylons and nightgowns, and I gave her a necklace for Christmas. She's a fine respectable girl. There's been nothing bad between us, no t'rills and grassing in the moonlight, nothing like that. Just my arm round her neck and a few kisses. That's all. And she says, 'Sammie, you're sweet.' "

Sam closed his eyes for a second of ecstacy, then shook his

head. "I don't know what to do about her; perhaps you could give me some advice. She wanted me to buy her a dress in the catalogue that cost ten dollars; I couldn't afford to keep a woman with such expensive taste as that. There's a couple of widows I might be able to git, they're older . . ." Sam rubbed his chin reflectively. "But the girl says, 'Sammie you're sweet,' and that makes me feel young and hansome. What do you think? She's twenty-four. Maybe she's too young for me; it might be like gas and water, they don't mix. She might want nothing but sex and new dresses and I want socks without holes and mashed potatoes."

Darkness came early. I found light and warmth in the Maclennans' kitchen. By the lamp on the table Elsa was mending; Alec was reading an old Halifax paper; Dougal, ten, to avoid being sent to bed, was being bright and attentive on the wood box.

"I saw the chalice today," I told them.

"Pretty thing, ain't it?" Alec said and gave me the story again.

"Did you see the *Ariadne,* Dad?" Dougal asked.

"No, darlin', I was just a lad and not living in the Harbour then." Alec turned towards me. "You know a funny thing about that wreck, they say a week before it happened one of the men from Neil's Harbour was at the place where the ship struck and he seemed to see a nigger swimming towards the land and sure enough when the *Ariadne* broke up a big black man was washed ashore and they buried him here."

"Did the man tell about seeing the swimmer before or after the wreck?" Elsa mused.

Alec laughed at her smartness, "You know, I never thought of that."

I asked about the treasure Matt Clipper and the old man talked about in the morning. "That would be Jordon's treasure," Alec said. "In those days the sailing vessels carried all their gold with them for trading; they'd come from the Indies loaded with molasses or rum, or made-goods from England, some come from far away with spices and coffee, figs and bananas. I don't know where the brigantine came from that carried Jordon's treasure, but she was on her way from Montreal where she had sold her cargo for wheat and fifty-six bags full of gold."

153

"Gold," Dougal echoed, his mouth round as a coin.

Alec smiled at his son. "Fifty pounds of pure gold in each bag," he said. "The brig was coming down the St. Lawrence to the Gulf and everything was fine. But the captain was a bad man and the mate no better; they wanted to get rid of the crew before they reached the sea so they landed on the Magdalines, sent some of the seamen ashore to look for water, then quickly sailed off without them. At St. Paul's Island they stopped again and made the rest get off."

"What happened to them?" Dougal asked.

"Maybe they died, I couldn't say, the islands are awful bare and this was a long time ago. Anyhow only the Captain, the mate and the cabin boy were left when she came past here with all sails set wing and wing. It was fine weather and they ran her careful between a cliff and a sunken rock, the split rock over there, they say," Alec pointed across the bay. "We know the rock must have been sixty feet high because they used a dipsy line on the yard-arm to unload the gold. After they buried it the Captain ordered the mate to go and look for civilization but as soon as he turned his back the Captain shot him dead. The cabin boy always claimed afterward that the Captain slipped between the ship and the rock and was drowned, but we think the lad got scared when he seen what happened to the mate and watched his chance to get rid of the Captain."

"Did he shoot him?" Dougal's eyes were popping.

"I don't know how he done it, he never told. There was a bara-chois nearby and some Frenchmen was there looking for moose, they found the lad and took him with them to Louisburg. He was only twelve year old and had no folks, he said, so they kept him in their homes to rear him up. He never told them about the trea-sure but sometimes when he was playing with their lads he'd tease 'em by saying, 'If you knew what I know you'd be rich!' and they used to wrestle with him to get it out of him but he never told where the gold was.

"In time he grew up and strayed away and nobody heard from him. But people round here never forgot the treasure and when they found out Jordon was in New York a couple of them went all the way down there to look for him. It wasn't such a big city then as it is now so they went to the Post Office and asked if

154

there was a man named Jordon that came in for his mail. Post Master said yes, a school teacher he was and came in every day. Next evening they waited by the wicket till Jordon turned up. They told him what they was there for and asked him to come with them and stand on the burying spot. He said no, he wouldn't have nothin' to do with it, too many was killed for it already. But he wrote out a map for them and said when they found the gold he'd like a share of it because he could do with a little money.

"My grandfather and one or two others round Cape North had the chart all writ out by Jordon himself. They were always claiming they knew right where to dig and they used to go in the night time so no one would know where they went and could get the treasure ahead of them. Always looking and talking about it they were, always digging somewhere in the dark, but never finding nothing."

"Maybe it's at Long Point, Daddy, there's a sixty-foot cliff there," Dougal was excited.

"No, darlin', Grandfather had Jordon's own map and he never went near Long Point," Alec said.

"Are there any other treasures?"

"There was Indians that camped in Grandfather's field and a squaw used to come to Grandfather's house, she'd stand in the doorway and say she was looking towards a river that was flowing with gold. It wasn't very far away, she said, and so thick she could cut it out with her tommy-hatchet. The way she found it, she said, was when she was washing her papoose's clothes and they come out of the water glinty with gold dust.

"Grandfather asked her to take him to the river but she kept putting him off. Then he tried to find it himself. He'd saddle his horse and go straight out from the door of his house as far as he could go in the direction she used to look. He'd crawl on his belly through the bush and come home scratched and bleeding. But it was no use. He'd beg the squaw to take him, he gave her eggs and bread and milk, he killed an ox and fed her whole tribe, he done all sorts of things for that squaw so she'd tell him where to find the golden river and he kept it up for years but she never told him and he never found it." Alec nodded sagely, "I guess she was a pretty artful woman."

155

"There are so many stories about treasures but nobody ever found one," Elsa remarked.

"Yes they did," Alec said, "Dick Mackay's grandfather did. He was just a poor farm hand once. He and another man were ploughing on an island near Ste. Anne's and their plough hit something that wouldn't budge. They thought it must be a rock so Mackay went forward to have a look and saw it was an iron chest, all rusty. He didn't tell the man working with him what he seen, just let him go home with the ox, said he'd stay and look after the plough.

"In the night time when there was nobody round, Mackay dug up the chest and it was full of gold. He left his plough right there in the field by the sea, never went near it again. He must have found plenty of money because he came here to the Cove right after that and started a business and the Mackays have been the richest people round here ever since."

"Tomorrow I'm going to dig somewhere," Dougal said.

CHAPTER EIGHTEEN

SEALS, CATS AND ART

SUNDAY, AUGUST 26

The rain is over, the sun shines, racing from the horizon are stallions with flying manes, they leap upon islets of granite and smash into fountains of spray; walls of transluscent jade are high as the hollowed bank, cream-crested, top-heavy, they curve, they fall into turquoise foam, seething, eddying, boiling round boulders dark with wet.

As the waves fly into spindrift, ecstacy bursts inside me. I'd like to shout loud as the deafening sea, as the roar of the breakers assaulting the land; I'd like to challenge the wind like the gulls that ride on its back.

I sit near the lighthouse and watch and listen and dream – and I wonder, "How can I tell this? How can the sea in a storm be imagined by those who have never been near it? Far inland I've heard people say – I've said it myself – 'We don't need to go to the ocean, we have the Great Lakes, they're practically the same, you can't see land across them, they get terribly rough in a gale.' "

True. The lakes are certainly fine, but compared with the

157

ocean they slap their shores with the force of a landlocked bay. At Neil's Harbour every billow has the power of the watery depths that circle the globe; when one wave lashes the land all the seas of the world have moved it.

Molly saw me on the Point. "Aren't you going to church?" I asked her.

"I goes in early morning when they's not so many people. I sets where I can see the candles burning. It makes me feel right holy." Molly's face has the bloom of a buttercup. "Jesus jumpins," she suddenly cried, "you better hurry or bell will be ringin'."

"I can't go, I haven't a hat."

"Foolish to matter, ain't it? Coom wi' me and I'll let you have my new one got this year from the catalogue." Molly's flower-trimmed red straw wasn't happy on my head but it gave me the respectability I needed to sit on the back bench of the little chapel.

Words and laughter died on the lips of everyone crossing the threshold. Children, important in Sunday clothes, bustled to their seats; women shyly straggled in alone; last came the men, wearing suits with cotton shirts open at the throat, they pulled off their caps in the doorway and crossed the creaking floor to their pews. Then for the first time I saw the bare heads of the fishermen. And almost all of them were bald!

On a low platform the minister stood behind a lectern, his wife played the hand organ and three women on chairs against the front wall sang louder than the rest. The service was simple and not overlong. People lingered after it to chat in the church yard.

I walked down the road with Arlie. We watched terns flying over the waves. "Member dat bird I ketched?" he asked me.

"That was the first time I saw you."

A flash of smile showed Arlie's pleasure. " 'e were a steern and steerns ain't no good for nothin'."

"They look nice."

"Can't tame 'en though," he said. "Crows is the bestest." Arlie looked at me anxiously, "You got crows?"

"Lots of crows,"

He smiled with relief. "Sometoimes we finds deir nestes and gits baby crows and teaches 'em how to talk."

"The way you do?"

"Yis," he said, "and dey curses real good too."

The Malcolms' kitchen door was closed today to keep out the wind; the old woman's chair was drawn close to the stove. "Winter is coming and I am far from home," she said. Miss Laurie patted her shoulder, "Mother dear, you are home."

"I am far from the home I had in Ingonish when my mother was living." She glared at Miss Laurie then went on serenely, "We had a lovely house till the fire came and destroyed it; the flames swept behind all the houses in the village but only our's was taken."

"She's always talking about when she was a girl," Katie complained.

"I worked hard when I was a girl," the old lady went on, "I worked with a good many families, shifting around from one to another. A woman at Skir Dhu was as kind as she could be: I'd be out in the moonlight digging potatoes till she called me to go to bed. On Monday morning I'd go down in the darkness, put the clothes in the tub, and draw buckets of water from the brook running into the sea." She rocked placidly for a moment. "After my mother died we came to Neil's Harbour. It was a nice place then with lights along the shore where the Scotch people stayed in summer. They were such friendly people."

The old lady rocked for a while without speaking. Miss Laurie, sitting on the chair by the window, said, "I see Mrs. Kendall coming up the road, wonder where she's going on a day like this?"

Katie, looking over Laurie's shoulder, said, "Her legs are so thick round the ankles they seem to be put on upside down, don't they?"

"No one else out today, too windy."

"I don't like the wind," the old lady started again, "I didn't used to mind it but now it's a terrible thing." She rubbed her hands together. "The rings have come off my fingers, they've shrunk so small. It's bad to let yourself grow old; my father was never old, he drowned when I was a little girl." The old lady smiled faintly, "I wish they'd put me on the drift ice one day and let me float away." Her head drooped and she was dozing.

Katie noticed, "Laurie, now's your chance to slip over to Elsa's, you haven't left the house all week."

"I don't want to go now, it's too windy," Miss Laurie's hands were folded in her lap, her face had a look of contentment.

The window rattles in the frame, something is banging in another room, there is a whistle in the eaves, the walls shake when a violent gust attacks them. I cannot rest this afternoon.

I run into the gale, count the waves that lash the wharf, run past when the seventh has drenched it. Alone I sit on the sheltered side and look at the lonely village. How can I leave it? How can I go? Terns flash over the white-rimmed shore of the bay; on the water below me a large black bird with a cruel bill searches my face with red-rimmed eyes. Sam Hatch walks on the edge of the cliff; is he thinking of Eternity? The boats drawn up between the stages are a lifeless tangle of rigging, their dignity left in the sea. Heavy clouds press down on the mountains, the wind whips my hair across my face, I hug my arms to warm them.

Where is my morning exultation? Where is the power and the glory?

Racing the breakers to land, I was greeted by Matt Clipper from the dark doorway of a stage. "Wondered how long you'd set out there," he said, and his kindly soft voice cheered me.

"Some windy, ain't it?" He grinned. "Wind's near cold enough to shave ye, but this really ain't nothin', worst gales is round sealing toime."

"When's that?"

"Seals come round on drift hice, whelps come on eighth or ninth o' March but you ain't supposed to touch 'em till the fifteenth."

"How do you get them?"

"We goes out after 'em in boat, there's just loike roads and lakes o' water in the hice, and we pushes through, sometoimes drifts crashes together and if your boat is between it's crushed to kindlin' wood."

"And what happens to you?"

"Could be in it but we's mostly crawlin' or walkin' round on the hice after seals. You should see the little ones, you'd loike 'em, they's just loike a choild; when you come near to 'em they puts up their little paws – flippers we calls 'em – jest loike they wants weens loike a baby." Matt closed his eyes and shook his head. you to pick 'em up. They look at ye with big round heyess and "Oi couldn't kill 'em atall. They feeds on the mother and sucks the clear green hice; they's full growed in five days, never seen

160

anything loike it how them things grow. Mostly just the young men goes after 'em, they knocks 'em on head with a bat."

"Do they get many?"

"Sometoimes there's a great lot, one boat with two men gits maybe a hundred and fifty in a year. We only takes the young ones, they weighs from sixty to eighty pounds; the mothers go six hundred and is near fifteen feet long – big as them boats down there the fattest of 'em is. We skins 'em and sells 'em at two dollars a pelt; oil from 'em is whoite and clean when it's melted out and the meat is good to eat."

"Is the fur nice?"

"Waterproof and roight strong, can't never wear out. People has coats made from 'em. Dick Mackay over in Cove got one, looks roight foine too. That's what you should have."

"Right now," I said and ran for the shelter of the Malcolms' house, where the wind seemed to blow through the walls of my little bedroom and I kept wondering how a coat made of Neil's Harbour seals would be to wear in winter at home.

The only way to find out was to go boldly to the Cove and ask to see Mr. Mackay's, though I hadn't met the family, whom the fishermen speak of as set-apart, lords-of-the-manor sort of people from whom a friendly word is an experience to be boasted about. The older Mackay children go to university and Mr. and Mrs. Mackay often travel to Sydney and even farther in their black sedan.

With some misgiving I walked over to the Cove to ask the favour. The Mackay canning factory, surrounded by the Mackay warehouses, is at the bottom of the hill. Across the road is the Mackay store, larger than the ones in the Harbour, with neat, well-stock shelves where one day I had tried unsuccessfully to buy film and was waited on by a man – no doubt Mr. Mackay – who was unlike any man I had encountered in northern Cape Breton: he wore a white shirt with a starched collar, a tie kept in place with a clip, a suit made of striped worsted, well pressed. He looked like a prosperous city businessman and his manner of speaking took me back to the world of impersonal living.

The Mackays' clapboard house was larger than any other in the Cove and the only one not surrounded by a fence. The front porch being barricaded by a baby's folding gate, I went round to the back door and knocked.

A tall cheery woman seemed delighted to see me. "Come in, dear," she said when I told her why I had come, "but don't notice my kitchen. There are eleven of us now that the boys are home," she smiled happily. We passed through the large room where diapers were drying around the coal stove and a young girl was sweeping, into a dining room with a shining wood floor, through a small conventional living room to a bedroom from whose crowded closet Mrs. Mackay extricated the seal coat.

Its fur was short, crisp, mottled yellow-grey and brown, the skin stiff and heavy. "A perfect coat for a man," she said. "Dick wears it in all kinds of weather when he's out in the cutter, but a girl wants something softer, don't you think?" Then she showed me coats she'd cut down and made over for the younger children. She brought out her own coat, a well-worn muskrat. "My daughters tell me I should get a new one," she said, "but this is warm and I like it." The wealthiest woman stroked the undyed fur of the old-fashioned shawl collar. "I don't think I'd feel right in anything else, I've worn this for thirty years."

Molly and a city-looking girl were sitting on the stoop when I came back from the Cove. I gathered by inference that the stranger was Molly's husband's sister Inez, married to a bus driver in Halifax. They were watching an artist who had set up an easel beside the road. "What he doos there now, be that coloured?" Molly wondered.

"Of course," Inez said. The artist dabbled a bit on his pallette then touched his sketch with his brush.

"What do 'e do wi' them pitchers when they's finished?" Molly asked.

"He sells them, of course," Inez told her.

"Naw, surely nobody'd buy them things with stages and wharf and fishin' boats onto 'em?"

"I've seen 'em in stores in Halifax; people pay a lot to get 'em hand-painted," Inez said. "That's art."

"Gohd, they don't look good to me. Whoi they's roight rough when they gits done with 'em." Molly walked towards the artist then back again to us. "See how 'e doos it, 'e squeezes paint out o' tubes and just smears it on."

"They get good money for 'em," Inez insisted.

Molly plunked herself on the stoop. "Well Oi wouldn't want

162

'em no matter what they's worth," she said. "Ain't nothin' to 'em. None o' the artists Oi ever seen round 'ere could do it as good as the calendars. Oi wouldn't trade no hand-painted pitchers for that calendar I got over the kitchen sink."

"Oh Molly, that's no good," Inez said disgustedly. "You got that from the fish company for nothing."

"That's roight, and it's got the sweetest pitcher of a mother and a baby onto it that Oi ever seen."

"But it's not art," Inez objected.

"Whoi ain't it?" Molly demanded. "In the first place wouldn't it have to be drew?"

By the time I left Molly and Inez the artist had moved his easel farther along the road where he'd parked his car and was painting the boats in the bay. Children formed a half circle behind him until he chased them away. "What are you doing in this place?" he asked pleasantly when he saw me watching, and after we'd chatted awhile he said, "I don't see how you can admire these people, they live on one of the most beautiful coasts in the world but they have no appreciation of it whatever."

He opened the trunk of his car and showed me the sketches he'd done in Ingonish and the Harbour. There were none of the coastline alone: every picture had in it some of the things that the fishermen had made and used and left lying around in interesting, colourful patterns. The one he liked best had Molly's daily washing on a line: red, yellow, white and faded green against her rusty old house, the sea blue as indigo behind it and a huge golden woodpile beside. "While I was painting this," the man said, "a young woman with a Mona Lisa smile and the sweetness of a Raphael Madonna sat on the stoop nursing her baby. I'd make a fortune if I could get her on canvas the way I saw her."

On my way home for supper Calvin Leaf called to me; he was sitting against the wall of his dusty dark sawmill with his cat on his lap. "Look Aidna, look at this: 'e's claws is all pulled out that front paw, and 'is cheek is swole roight bad, see? 'is ears is nicked and seems loike somethin' hurt his back too. Don't know what I can do fer 'im, do you?" The old cat looked up at Calvin, his face not unlike Calvin's round stubbly one. "Pore kitty, 'e was a awful pretty cat." Calvin looked down affectionately. "By Christmas time 'e's fat and 'is fur's roight t'ick; it gits stuck together in gert wads and I got to clip it off – that's only way I can do with it," Calvin stroked it gently. "Oh the dear kitty cat, 'e's awful noice cat.

"I had 'e since year of the gert snow, snowed roight over top them windows, all ye need do to git water was rise 'em up and take in shovelful snow and put in bucket. I often seen cat with big bushy tail goin' in under sawmill but 'e wouldn't let me come handy to 'im. One day when I rised up the window 'e jumped roight up. I picked 'im off sill and 'e put 'is claws in me so I had a devil's toime gettin' clair of 'im, 'e fastened roight onto me. When I got 'im off I put 'im out door but 'e kep' comin' back and I feeded 'im and 'e been 'ere ever sence, best pet ever I had."

Calvin rubbed his cat's ears. "I near losed 'e one other toime. Couldn't foind 'im fer couple days, I called, 'Kitty, kitty,' and looked all round but nobody'd seed 'im. That evenin' I puts foire in stove to cook me sausingers; jest fer nothin' I opened oven door –don't know what maked me do it – and there was cat, 'e jumped roight out, pore t'ing could been roasted."

The wind went down with the setting sun; two snapper boats came back from Dingwall. While I was sitting on my fence rail the yellow dorys tied to the wharf shone bright as the sun's long rays struck them broadside; the sea was sapphire blue; the Light gleamed white against the sky. The only living creatures in sight were the hens, Alec's wild kittens and a cow.

But soon a rosy-cheeked little girl wearing a kerchief and scarlet jacket came up the road with a pickle jar of milk in the crook of her arm. "Dandy day," Mr. Battersey ceremoniously touched his homburg and stopped to chat: exasperatingly polite, he talked about the weather and his wife's operation; no matter how I have encouraged him he has never told me any of his exaggerated tales.

"Well, Edna, what a place to set!" The hearty voice was Ella Jane's as she walked hand in hand with little Dolly. "Whoi don't ye come up to the house where you can set comf'table? I thought maybe you was gone when ye never comed up the hill again."

"Have you heard from Maggie?"

"She got there, says Toronto's awful noisy and nobody knows nobody else nor cares."

"She had a ride in a car," Dolly told me.

164

"Maggie'd loike that roight foine, but she'll foind out it ain't so handy as home."

Gordie came running down the hill towards us. "Mom, where's the hammer at?" he called. "She-cat got in the storehouse and spilled all the milk; some savage 'e was, spittin' like a squid."

"That cat's so thievin' she'd steal the eyes roight out o' yer head. How'd she git in there?"

"Musta followed somebody and then got barred in; she busted the screen to git out and Dad wants to fix it but can't foind where the hammer's at."

"Lord God Almighty, that's an awful man, that is, can't let me go nowhere without sendin' after me. Me and Doll was goin' to see poor Hattie, ain't been in there since they carried him out. Now I guess I got to go up the hill again and clean up that milk."

I heard a whistle and a shout; it came from Sam Hatch, who lives across the road from my reception rail in an unpainted house where one gable has been removed and the wall patched with boards painted pink, a brown door on one side, a blue one on the other and the front door apple green. Sam asked me to come over. "I'd like to give you a souvenir of Neil's Harbour," he said, holding up a huge slab of mica. Impossible to carry from boats to buses to trains with all my luggage. I said, "You're much too generous, you shouldn't give me such a big piece."

"Oh I got plenty, there's a whole mountain of it, all shiny black, eight miles back," he pointed towards the Trail.

"Queer flakey stuff, isn't it? Would break up easily, wouldn't it?"

"This piece is right solid, you don't need worry about it breaking." He lifted it over the pickets that were between us and dropped it into my arms. The weight made me founder. "Heavy, ain't it?" Sam said.

I could hardly hold it. I didn't want to hurt the man's feelings, but I had to say, "I'm afraid I can't carry this."

"I'll be glad to take it down to Malcolms' for you."

"Please don't," I cried as he started along the fence to the gate, "could you give me a smaller piece to remember you by, something I could put in my pocket?"

He took the slab from me, "I got plenty little pieces, I just didn't want you to think I was stingy."

CHAPTER NINETEEN

CAUGHT MY FISH

MONDAY, AUGUST 27

Katie packed a lunch for me early this morning and I ran down the shore where the swordfishermen were gathering. Their mass no longer scared me; faces I knew smiled as I came along.

The boats were jammed between the stages – useless and awkward out of the water. Pealed saplings made a runway over the stones. The men pushed on either side of each boat till sixteen boats were back in the sea. "Calvin don't want his in, says he's givin' up fishin' fer a spell," Big Jim grinned at me.

I waited on the wharf for the men to come to the two snapper boats. The first one refused me, "Sorry, Edna, we got an extra man today." The soldier was with them. All the small boats had gone. Only the *Carlotta,* the smallest snapper boat, was left at her mooring. Three men came out from the shore, men I didn't know: one was very big, one very young, the other, older with

166

red eyebrows and warm brown eyes. "Would you like to have a passenger?" I asked them.

"Woman aboard's bad luck," the big man muttered.

"I'm good luck, you'll see, I'll bring you good luck, I feel awfully lucky today."

The men looked at each other, the older one said, "We been at it two months and ain't got but three..."

"All right then, Kootch, let 'er come," said the big man.

I scrambled atop the fo'c'sle before the engine was started. Diddle, the big man, and Gerald, his son, climbed the mast; when the *Carlotta* was moving, Kootch sat on the fo'c'sle near me. The sea was like watered silk, a hundred boats slipped over it like skaters on a rink.

"Ever seen one o' these?" Kootch handed me a double-barbed dart of bronze and explained that it was socketed in the end of the harpoon by keeping taut along the pole the strong line that ran to a coil in a box amidships with an initialed red keg tied at the end of the hundreds of feet of line. The keg could be thrown into the water to mark and retard a wounded fish. "But we don't take no chances of a big one pullin' kag down under and burstin' it," Kootch said. "We lower dory quick and start playin' him afore 'e gits off. Sometimes they're too smart for us though and we got to throw a keg over; then might be they get right away with it or another boat picks up our fish."

All the time he was talking Kootch kept watching the water and I kept watching it too. I was a veteran sailor, I had no fear of the sea; on this trip I was really alert. "Look, look," I cried, "a FISH!"

And so it was – a shark.

We were going towards Cape North. Kootch moved to the front of the fo'c'sle, I sat crosslegged behind him. We turned south towards Smokey. We headed towards the horizon to ride great sweeps of water as placidly as ducklings ride a ripple in a pond. A breeze came up and the water was ruffled, we turned again to the south. For an hour we kept moving, then Diddle on the mast yelled, "FISH!"

Kootch ran out on the rigging. The fish was much too close, the pulpit was past it before the harpoon could be lifted. The *Carlotta* was turned round sharply to come back to stab the fish.

But the fins had disappeared.

Kootch stayed out in the pulpit while we circled the water like bird dogs on a scent. Then Kootch shook his head and came back to sit again on the fo'c'sle.

We took a straight course to the north. The breeze was certainly freshening. We passed the clearing of Neil's Harbour; we passed the outlet of the Cove. Kootch lit a fire in the fo'c'sle and the men took turns to eat. I had my lunch on the roof so I wouldn't miss a fish. We saw the mountain ridge that protects the harbour at Dingwall. We turned again towards the south. Boats were everywhere round us, restlessly moving and searching.

Near us, one of the boats had stopped with its dory almost alongside. In the little boat were two men, the one standing seemed to be pulling a line, the other, crouched over, was bailing fast as he could. "Must ha' been struck," Kootch shouted towards our mast.

"They're gettin' their fish," Diddle answered.

"They ain't in no danger," Kootch told me. "Fish musta struck afore big boat got away and other fella went in dory to bail." Then he explained: "Swordfish is quiet resting fish, wouldn't hurt nobody if they's left alone. Swords is made for slashing, not stabbing; but sometimes when a fish is hit near the head 'e goes crazy like and turns on boat or dory. He can ram 'is sword clear through a two-inch plank, 'e could splinter a thinner boat and a man if 'e's in the way. Sword usually breaks off and fish dies quick after that, but a man could die quick too if he's stabbed or gits himself tangled in a line and dragged down. Never seen it happen yet though, just heard of it."

The breeze was becoming a wind, the *Carlotta* took the water like a broncho. I sat closer to the mast. We went down past Ingonish Island, past Middle Head, almost as far as Smokey, then far out to sea where our boat leapt and fell in the swells, a wonderful proud thing to feel. And all the time we kept watching for the precious stick-like fins. We saw several sharks, we saw dolphin, we saw a blackfish blow. The wind was growing colder.

Diddle's voice roared, "FISH!"

Kootch ran out to the pulpit.

"Port," Gerald called and we saw the fins in the water.

Diddle steered straight towards the prize. The motor stopped.

168

We were quiet. Tense. We were close. Kootch held the harpoon in his hand. The fish was almost alongside. "Oh God, get 'im, get 'im," I prayed.

Kootch lunged. The fish was gone. The pole fell slack in the water. Kootch jerked it back to the pulpit.

Diddle came down from the mast with Gerald tumbling after. "Stuck 'im right behind front fin," Diddle called as he grabbed the line uncoiling from the box amidships.

Kootch rushed to the stern, the dory was lowered and Diddle jumped into it with the keg and box in his arms. Quickly he tautened the line with the dart on the end in the fish.

" 'e's on," Diddle shouted, " 'e's on," and at once was jerked away by the plunging wounded swordfish.

We watched him go. Without the steadying drive of the motor, the *Carlotta* was seesawing madly. I clung to the mast. Kootch grinned at me as he passed on his way to the pulpit to put a new dart in the pole. Gerald started the motor and we were moving again. Kootch's place on the front of the fo'c'sle was constantly splashed as we plunged into deepening waves. "Worst swell I ever were out in," he said as he moved back and sat beside me.

"What are we going to do now?" I asked him.

"Look for another fish till Diddle gits that one played out."

We didn't go far from Diddle; except when he was hidden by waves we always kept him in sight. He stood in the little dory, pulling in line and letting it out as the swordfish tried to escape him by riding him round in the sea.

"Looks like 'e might be a big one," Kootch said when we'd circled for almost an hour. He seldom watched the loppy water for another fish, he kept turning anxious glances towards the yellow dory. "Sometimes we loses a fish," he said. "Sometimes it takes three-four hours to tire out a big one. Sometimes a fish will turn on a dory before 'e dies."

As we kept moving east, south, west and north, all the other fishing boats were going in one direction, all going towards a harbour. Soon we were alone on the ocean with the little yellow dory. The hill of water towards the horizon seemed steeper than it had in the morning, the land seemed farther away. "Wind's right nardly now," Kootch said.

169

It was useless to pretend we were looking for another fish, we kept our eyes on Diddle. He was pulling on the line, letting it out, pulling it in, letting it out as he stood in the little boat.

For a lonely hour we circled.

Then Diddle raised his arm. We rushed to the dory heaving up and down in the waves. Diddle was smiling broadly, the water around him was red, the great curved tail of the swordfish was securely tied to the thwart.

Diddle clambered into the *Carlotta*. With the help of a tackle the fish was hauled aboard. It stretched across the full width of the boat with its head running up the side, its sword above the gunwale. "Not the biggest one I ever seen in my life," was the first comment Kootch made, "but 'e'll go seven hundred pound." He thumped Diddle's shoulder with joy.

"'e was a dirty little bastard," Diddle said. "Wouldn't go up or down, kep' hittin' the rope with 'is tail." He was grinning; Kootch was grinning too and so were Gerald and I.

"You's lucky," Diddle said to me, "you can git a ship any time now. Jesus Christ, they'll all be beggin' ye to go with them!"

They hauled in the dory, the men climbed the mast, Kootch sat on the engine door, I sat on the little bench. The *Carlotta* leaped towards the Harbour.

We rode straight up to the fish dock. A crowd was there to see. Kootch fastened a rope round the swordfish tail and the men on the wharf pulled it up.

"OOOOOOOOOOO, a good one, a good one," everyone said in a way that was almost a cheer. For a blessed moment the great fish hung high, then they let it down with a *plop*.

As we followed it over the rail Diddle announced in his booming voice, "This girl's good luck, we want her to ship with we, everybody else can't have her."

Kootch and Gerald moored the *Carlotta* and Diddle gutted our catch. The sword was a trophy for me. Diddle said, "Guess you'll sure want to take that one home."

Home!

I had caught my fish and would have to go home. The little man who weighs the fish told me the *Aspy* was missing a trip this week but the fish boat would be in early tomorrow morning. And I would be leaving Neil's Harbour.

The dock was swarming with men, children, dogs, fish and Molly, all in a great state of glee. Someone had brought in a porpoise and everyone wanted to see it. "Funny lookin' ting, ain't 'e?" Uncle Joe said. "They follows boat loike a dog."

"Ain't got no heyess," said one of the children.

"Yis 'e do, see 'ere roight behind 'is mouth," Molly said, "small though."

"See this hole on top, that's where 'e breathes. 'e comes on top water and blows just loike a whale," Uncle Joe told us.

"Look at 'is tongue," said Molly, "just loike a cat, and did yer ever see such teeth, set in loike on combs."

"Smooth skin, ain't it?" Freddie kneeled beside the fish.

"Not loike swordfish," Molly said. "Rub yer hand on swordfish and it'll take yer skin roight off so ye need a plaster, Arlie done it with 'is arm and it drawed blood."

"Skin's an inch t'ick," said Uncle Joe.

"Is he good to eat?" Gwendoline asked.

"They says so," Uncle Joe answered. "Tastes loike piece o' beef."

"Boi Cheesus 'e stinks loike 'e's rotten," Molly held her nose. "Oi wouldn't want 'im fer moi kids."

I walked on the Point in the moonlight. As one does not look at the sun to enjoy the sunlight, so in Neil's Harbour one does not look at the moon, but becomes absorbed by its gleaming on the living water, its dimming of the yellow flame of the Light, its cold brilliance on the stages in whose shadows one feels warm. I could see the faces of the houses in the cool white light, all looking in one direction, all looking at the sea where the fishing boats come in; all but the houses of the doctor, the preacher, the merchants, whose places face the road because they have no men coming into the harbour.

I watched the moonpath on the water, living and breathing, silhouetting the little boats that lay in its wake, and sadly I thought: there is no moonpath in the city, there is no moonlight, no soft diffusion of blue brightness; there is only the moon, a disc of silver unnoticed above the electric spatters that light the streets in long monotonous rows.

CHAPTER TWENTY

YE CAN'T GIT AWAY FROM IT

TUESDAY, AUGUST 28

This is a sad day: this is the day I'll be leaving Neil's Harbour.

I packed my bags at half past six and ran down to the shore to say goodbye to my friends before they went out fishing.

They laughed at me. They wouldn't believe I was going. "This ain't first toime you said you was off," Jim Clipper said, "this will be just loike all the rest. Calvin won't let you git away."

"Moight be fish boat won't come today," Leo spoke.

"You'll be here when we gits in," Jack Seaforth smiled. "You won't be leavin' fer a spell yet."

They shuffled down to their dories. I sat on the dock and watched them go out on the sea.

The *sea*. How can I leave it? And how can I leave the Harbour for streets and buildings, speed and clatter, cocktails and chit-chat? Surrounded by comfort and noise and the pleasant people

I love, I suppose all this will seem as if it had never been. At home as I talk and laugh – and take baths – I'll have to try to remember how the sea broke on the rocks, how the people reached the houses on the hill, what Matt Clipper's voice was like, how Miss Laurie gently served her mother and her cow.

"OOOO look, holy cheesus, look at the big Johnnie crab, I'm goin' roll up and go in after he." Hector rolls up his pants and wades into the water beside the dock. He carries a pole and he screams in the icy coldness. None of the other children who have come to the wharf pay him attention as they lean over the edge to see what treasures the tide has washed in.

"Arlie, come 'ere, Arlie, my son," Freddie shouts to his brother, "just come and look at the son of a bitch of a skulkin 'ere."

"Git 'im, Freddie, git – oh ye near went owerboard."

Freddie looks at me and grins, "Water's some cold down dere."

Looking down I see olive-brown kelp gently swaying, the soft green leaves of a sea-fern, feathery little shrubs with pearly blue buds shining in filtered sunlight; I see dark shadows of perch and an awkward crawling lobster fastening to a piece of fish gut.

"Hector why don't ye git that Johnnie crab?" Arlie asks.

"I can't git en, my son, 'e's gone."

"Come and see sniles 'angin' on 'ere, they's roight aloive," Arlie leans over the side. He looks up at me, "If Oi slips . . ."

"If you slips, you slips," warns Freddie.

"Oww, I got me shirt wet," wails Hector, now under the dock.

Four-year-old Bobbie yells, "Hector, dear, look at Johnnie crab, 'e's goin' on yer toe."

"Son of a bitch, the little goddam barstid," Hector shakes his foot.

"Don't splash me, Hector, ye barstid," Bobbie runs away from the commotion but comes right back. "Cheesus, why don't ye kill them Johnnie crabs?"

"Me toe's bleedin'," Hector wails.

"Crabs be roight wicked, hides under rocks and then comes out and gits ye," Arlie tells me. "They runs sideways."

Hector goes into action. He plunges his pole in the water, he strikes at everything that moves. "Now I got one, I got one," he shouts with glee, and from between the planks of the dock I feel a jab in the part of me that is – was – sitting.

Molly was watching a caterpillar in front of her house. "Seems to know where 'e's goin' don't 'e?" she said as I came along. The thickly furred little rectangle undulating among the pebbles on the road was purposefully moving in a straight line.

"You'd wonder what makes him go like that, wouldn't you?"

"Yis, ain't nothin' inside but green juice," Molly said thoughtfully. "Main thing I guess is he's aloive." She got up to see him more closely. "Looks roight good on outside, don't 'e?" The bit of brown fur made a right turn. "Changed 'is moind!" Molly exclaimed. "Ain't that funny now, whoi 'e doos that?"

We watched the caterpillar till it went under a plank then Molly said, "Lotsa queer critters in world, ain't there?" She looked at me quizzically. "Sometoimes I thinks even we's some queer, don't you?"

I sat for a while with Molly and watched for the fish boat to come. We didn't talk, we just sat there and looked at the sea and the sky.

I ran up the road to Elsa, then into the store to Alec. "No use sayin' goodbye till the boat's here, it may not come till tomorrow," he said as he firmly clasped my hand. "I can't believe you're leavin' and even if you are you'll be back."

I was on the ramp of Tom Candle's stage after dinner when we saw the fish boat come. "What for are you goin'?" Tom asked me. "Why don't ye git a man here? I know one or two might have ye." He sent Tommy and Kennie to the house with me to carry my bags to the dock.

Katie had gone picking berries. I left *War and Peace* for her; the mother smiled as she said she was glad I had come and she hoped I'd enjoy my visit; Miss Laurie kissed me and wistfully said, "You'll write to us, won't you, dear? It's lonely here all winter." Then shyly she gave me a folded page and told me to read it when I was on my way.

Matt Clipper was down on the wharf. "Oi can hardly believe you're leavin'," he said when I gave him my hand, "and Oi don't roightly think that you are, ye loikes the Harbour too well. You can't git away from a place that you're fond of. You'll keep com-

in' back in your moind and first thing ye know you'll be with us."
His blue eyes looked far at the sea. "Oi went away once, shipped on boat for Boston; but Oi couldn't stick it, kep' thinkin'
about folk here, kep' hearin' their voices till it was just loike
they was callin' me back. Oi never got very far, Oi turned round
and come home." He smiled at me. "You'll see that's how it will
be fer you if you git out on that fish boat. It won't be long you'll
be back in Neil's Harbour."

"But I don't live here, my home is inland, my people are there
and they want me."

Matt's face was troubled. "It will be hard fer you," he said,
"but Oi know the spell o' the sea is on you. Ye can't never git
away from that. And you's fallen in love with the Harbour just
loike you's got you a man. People 'ere want ye too and we need
ye, we'd loike fer ye to learn our children in school. Oi told trustees moight be ye'd come and do it, so git aboard now, go home
quick and fetch back yer gear."

Then I was on the bilgey old fish boat. At last I was on my way,
passing the shores beyond Green Cove, the Harbour was soon
out of sight.

Till I could see it no longer I stood in the stern and waved. I
waved to Miss Laurie on her white porch, to Sam Hatch walking
along the cliff, to Nellie Williams on the Road, to Alec in the
doorway of the store, to Elsa, to Charlotte, Ella Jane, and Molly in their yards facing the sea, to Tom Candle, Matt Clipper,
Henry Rider, Calvin and his cats, the children, and the codfishermen waving at me from the shore and the fish dock. I
waved goodbye to all the little houses, the clustered stages, to
the Light against the sky.

Then I opened Miss Laurie's paper and read:

A stranger from inland wandered one day into Neil's Har-
bour and wanted to stay,
She came on our porch, peeping in through the screen, she
pleadingly said, "Can you take me in?"
She looked like a laddie in her summer dress but round her
hung many a long curling tress.
We talked for a minute and then I did say, "How long, may
I ask, would you want here to stay?"

175

"How long?" she queried, "I just do not know, depends on
my liking how soon I may go."

We then let her in and showed her a room, to every appear-
ance she seemed quite at home.

Day in and day out she returned to the shore and gathered
yarns from the fishermen's store.

She swam the Atlantic and rode on its crest, in the snapper *Carlotta,* one of the best,

She strolled on the deck like a son of the main, she saw
the bold swordfish harpooned and slain.

When three weeks were over she made up her mind, to return to her home leaving new friends behind.

We'll miss you, dear girl, and this wish we give, May you
be happy and long may you live."